D0053900

Historians
and the Law in
Postrevolutionary
France

1. Cour de Cassation, Galerie des Magistrats et Jurisconsultes.
From André Dupin, *Eloge des douze magistrats*. Photograph courtesy
of Bibliothèque Nationale.

DONALD R. KELLEY

Historians
and the Law in
Postrevolutionary
France

PRINCETON UNIVERSITY PRESS
PRINCETON, NEW JERSEY

Copyright © 1984 by Princeton University Press
Published by Princeton University Press,
41 William Street, Princeton, New Jersey 08540
In the United Kingdom:
Princeton University Press,
Guildford, Surrey

Library of Congress Cataloging in Publication Data
will be found on the last printed page of this book
ISBN 0-691-05428-2

Publication of this book has been aided by
the Paul Mellon Fund of Princeton University Press
This book has been composed in Linotron Janson

Clothbound editions of Princeton University Press books
are printed on acid-free paper, and binding materials
are chosen for strength and durability

Printed in the United States of America
by Princeton University Press
Princeton, New Jersey

CONTENTS

LIST OF ILLUSTRATIONS

ACKNOWLEDGMENTS

It may seem rash for a *seiziémiste* to begin poaching on the territory of *l'histoire contemporaine*, but in fact I have not strayed far from the intellectual tradition that has interested me since an undergraduate infatuation with Lord Acton. Several of the authors discussed in the following pages I encountered in the secondary bibliography of earlier studies, and in general the legacy of the Old Regime still weighs heavily in the present work, though I have happily been able to escape some of its demands. On the whole, this has been a labor of pleasure, taking me on a tour of German as well as French libraries and intellectual landscapes either familiar or forgotten, thanks in part to a grant from the American Philosophical Society. I owe something to my elders and betters in this field—I think especially of Sanford Elwitt, Charles Freedeman, John Salmon, and Ralph Giesey—but in this case I'm not sure just what. I must thank Stanley Mellon for his critical reading of the original manuscript, Miriam Brokaw and Sandy Thatcher for their critical encouragement, and Helen Hull, Jean Degroat, and Barb Stump for their patient technical assistance. The book, however, is for Bonnie—my Clio and my Themis, and likewise possessing an abundance of Patience.

30 June 1983
Rochester, N.Y.

Historians
and the Law in
Postrevolutionary
France

CHAPTER ONE

Clio and Themis

> Il faut éclairer l'histoire par les lois, et les lois
> par l'histoire.
> —Montesquieu (1748)

This is an essay in a rather specialized area of intellectual history, but it touches on larger concerns. One is the familiar point, argued and illustrated a generation and more ago by Herbert Butterfield and before him Lord Acton, that the history of historiography is more than an exercise in hagiography, a trivial version of the "Whig fallacy"; it is also a path to cultural self-criticism and self-understanding.[1] Of all scholars, historians should be least susceptible to that academic "amnesia" lamented by Sorokin that leads each generation to invent the wheel anew, to claim a novelty that on reflection turns out to be an old construct given a new dress.[2] Yet fashion and generational divergence seem to affect historiography almost as immediately as they have philosophy or literary criticism, despite irrepressible "scientific" claims.

How many faces has Clio shown us over the centuries? How many "new histories" have there been since La Popelinière's project of 1599? The claims have been many, and consistently grandiose. Not superficial events but deep structures of society, *Annalistes* have argued; not drums and trumpets but the life of the people, J. R. Green proclaimed; not just religion and politics but all of civilization, Voltaire pleaded, as James Harvey Robinson has done in our century.[3] In this book we encounter still another *histoire nouvelle*, whose novelty was likewise defined in invidious contrast to a prevailing style of historical writing perceived as narrow and inadequate. As with the other "new histories," however, we have paid too

3

much attention to the rhetoric and the pretensions of the conspicuous figures and not enough to the practice and accomplishments of their less visible or less fashionable colleagues. My first purpose is to take a closer look at this seminal period of historical scholarship, roughly the two generations between 1804 and 1848, and so to gain a better general perspective on the history of history.

Related to this is a still less appreciated point about the history of humanistic scholarship in general. This is a field, or set of fields, that should not be a mere chronicle of achievements catalogued within a narrow disciplinary framework, still less an uncritical record of programmatic statements and theoretical claims (another "new history," say) about humanity in general. Yet curiously and lamentably, the history of scholarship, and especially of historical scholarship, seems to be in its conceptual infancy compared to the history of science, philosophy, political thought, and even literature. In the past generation the history of science, for example, has been transformed from a chronicle to a critical stage—with discussions of "scientific revolutions" being the counterpart, perhaps, to new histories—and in many ways placed in social and cultural context.[4] By contrast history, which one would expect to be even more amenable to such treatment, has remained in an embarrassingly backward condition, especially because of its self-imposed isolation from philosophy and the social sciences (except in certain technical ways). Unreflective empiricism is the bane of historical understanding, and the widespread discredit that intellectual history has brought upon itself should not produce a contempt for theory or what Collingwood called "historical self-knowledge." Cut off from interdisciplinary awareness and from their own disciplinary past, historians may end up talking to themselves—and perhaps not listening.

Conspicuously, this was not the case in the first half of the nineteenth century, when "social science" (the term, anyway) was indeed novel, exciting, and enhancing, and when history itself was open and cordial to many other fields and international exchanges.[5] While much of the story of "Romantic" historiography has been told, at least in narrative fashion, there are aspects of it, substantive as well as conceptual, that remain obscure. Its narrative form has been studied with care and affection, but little attention has been paid to its analytical and interpretive depth; its "political uses" have been followed in some detail, but its social correlates hardly at all; its novelty has been celebrated at length, but its roots in and carry-overs from the Old Regime have been largely ignored. The present essay in interdisciplinary contact is intended to expand our view of this period of historical thought and scholarship on all of these counts.

It is tempting to bring some of the insights of Thomas Kuhn to bear upon the emergence of the "new history" of the Romantic age, or at least to the conceptual framework assumed by thinking historians. At the turn of the century the "normal science" of history had indeed reached a low point. Many young writers, most notably Augustin Thierry, saw the need for revitalization, for a "reconstruction" (Kuhn's term) within a new framework. In general, in the wake of the great Revolution, natural law concepts were proving illusory and impractical—"anomalous" with respect to historical and political experience. In the first quarter of the century there was a perceptible "crisis" in historical thinking that went beyond political reaction or changing sensibilities associated with Romanticism to a profound dissatisfaction with the shallow and utilitarian view of history inherited from the Enlightenment. Making the distinction between chronicle and true history, Thierry expressed his desire to "reproduce with fidelity the ideas, sentiments, and customs of the men who gave us the name we bear."[6] He wanted to look further into the depths of social history than anyone had done before and to see it with new eyes, and so did other young historians of his generation. The larger intellectual context of this enterprise was a general movement away from the abstract and lifeless mechanism, and equally abstract and lifeless empiricism, of old-fashioned natural law toward a biological and evolutionary model of perception and explanation. It would no doubt be an exaggeration to claim that the change of intellectual climate represented a "paradigm-shift" from naturalism to historicism. Still, the postrevolutionary period did witness the emergence of a more consciously historical cast of mind that was indeed the basis for historical reconstruction and much of the newness of the so-called new history of the second quarter of the century.

Even at second hand, however, I would not presume to demonstrate the structure of "historical revolutions" (though the term has been applied to the Romantic age by Acton and Thierry, among others). For one thing, I am persuaded that the intellectual continuities between the new and the old history were too extensive even for unqualified claims of "novelty," not to speak of "revolutionary" advance.[7] More important, perhaps, devotees of the new history of the Restoration period quite consciously took insights and inspiration from presumably outmoded authors, not only earlier innovators like Vico and Herder but also pre-"scientific" scholars of the Renaissance like Poliziano and Cujas. In any case, what is a controversial thesis even for the "hard" sciences can hardly be more than vaguely suggestive for a humanistic field like historiography and for a "new history" whose provenance was as much literary as philosophical, inspired as directly by Walter Scott and Chateaubriand as by Herder and Vico. My concern here is mainly to clarify the pattern of historical investigation and interpretation in the postrevolutionary age and to reveal what I believe to be the roots of that "scientific" history usually attributed to a later period. In particular, the establishment of institutional history on a solid and exhaustive documentary basis was accomplished in the environment, so to speak, not of Realism but of Romanticism, as indeed professional historians of the later nineteenth century were disposed to acknowledge.

Another distinction given currency in the debates over Kuhn's thesis—though in fact it was well established in the Romantic age and is traceable back at least to Leibniz—is that between "externalist" and "internalist" history.[8] Here I hope to throw some light on both aspects. For what early nine-teenth-century historians called "external history" I offer dis-cussions of the political, institutional, legal, and social heri-tage of the Revolution of 1789; of some of the relevant public issues, including the relationship between the legislative and the judiciary and the problems of private property; of the most articulate parts of the French intelligentsia, including lawyers and journalists as well as scholars; of the hopes, fears, and problems generated by the revolution of 1830; and of course of some of the principal published works associated with the new history. The "internal history" is represented by parallel discussions of conceptions of historical process and perspec-tive, of continuity and change, of the interconnections be-tween institutions, of the role of human values and human will, and especially of the doctrines of the German "historical schools." All of these factors go into an adequate account of a major intellectual transformation—if not "revolution"—which in the largest and most impressionistic terms is represented by the rise of "historicism," but is here defined more restrict-edly as a fundamental stage in the development of modern historical scholarship.

Before the Revolution, history had played at best an auxil-iary role in social and ideological controversies. The language of analysis and debate was dominated by "three competing vocabularies," according to Keith Baker, who defines them respectively as "political discourse," corresponding to govern-mental and legislative will; "judicial discourse," which in-voked ideals of justice; and "administrative discourse," which appealed to reason.[9] Both defenders and opponents of the monarchy argued in these terms and within the "political cul-ture" defined by them before 1789. A quarter of a century later, all three types of discourse seemed in a sense discred-ited, or at least exhausted. Royal "will" could never be fully resuscitated, administrative "reason" smacked of Bonapart-ism, and "justice" in any universal sense seemed a mockery to all but the direct beneficiaries of the Revolution, and even then only if they could maintain their share of the spoils. So

7

a new language had to be devised to accommodate the issues of Restoration and the new confrontations provoked after 1815. History seemed a promising access to the common ground of social experience, though of course there were as many readings and "meanings" of history as there were interest groups. How could historical discourse be given a focus for such a variety of political interests? How could historical perspective give definition to the urgent questions, much less the answers, of the postrevolutionary age?

Perhaps the most crucial point about the strategy of this book is the interdisciplinary emphasis, and this brings us back to another implication of the Kuhn thesis. In order to "see new things when looking at old objects," as Kuhn put it,[10] it is useful and perhaps necessary to bring different presumptions, methods, and values to bear upon a question. As Galileo looked at the problem of local motion with the eyes not of a natural philosopher but of a mathematician, so practitioners of the new history had to learn to look at the process of history with the eyes not of political chroniclers but of sensitive social critics. There were several places (including literature, political economy, and philosophy) where they could find new spectacles, but each of these fields presented problems. Philosophy still inclined to system, if not to idealism, as Goethe among others complained; and meanwhile the task of historiography, especially in Germany, was to extricate itself from this influence (the starting point, indeed, of Ranke's work). Political economy, at least the dominant liberal model, had preserved and was in the process of strengthening its ties with naturalism. Literature was most relevant, and in fact furnished a vital ingredient for the new history; but most historians (Michelet being a partial exception) were afraid that the siren song of poetry, or of imaginative fiction, would lead them astray.

Where then could they look? For a variety of reasons, the field of law seemed most promising because of its materials and methods. Jurisprudence still claimed to be a "science"— but of a human rather than natural variety—and was joined to a comprehensive view of anthropology that might accommodate a comparably encyclopedic vision of history. The careers of history and jurisprudence had of course converged more than once in earlier centuries (most notably in the context of the "new history" of the Renaissance), but the nineteenth century saw an intersection of unprecedented intensity and significance for both disciplines. It was, in a sense, the fulfillment of Montesquieu's hope that "history should illuminate laws, and laws history."[11] So it was that in the Romantic period, after what some regarded as a generation of lawlessness, the muse of history joined forces with Themis, goddess of human law.

I would point out four aspects of the law that made it fruitfully relevant for history: First, the law required and inspired respect for documentary evidence that led, especially in the nineteenth century, to that assault on archival sources so essential to the new science of history. Second, jurisprudence, in some ways even more than politics, was bound up with the most crucial public issues of the age, starting with the institution of property and ending with the Social Question, and so could join historical scholarship to vital contemporary issues, directly as well as indirectly. Moreover, the law was by its very nature concerned with the substance of history as envisioned by Thierry and others, namely, social institutions and the texture, structure, and processes of the private sector—the "civil society" that Hegel set apart from (and that Marx would set above) the state. Finally, the questions posed by jurisprudence in the post-Napoleonic age were absolutely central to the orientation of the new historiography, especially in the case of the debate over codification and the rival notion of law as an expression of popular culture (a sort of surrogate for the contrast between political and social history). It is an ironic, though perhaps it should be a commonplace, comment on the "novelty" of early nineteenth-century historical scholarship that it was in part a transformed extension of the old legal tradition.

The vitality of this scholarship is to be explained in terms of its international environment as well as its interdisciplinary roots. The Eclectic philosophy of Victor Cousin, the most influential professor of Restoration France, has not enjoyed good press in the past century and a half, but it was indicative of the formative influx of the foreign ideas and discoveries in the early nineteenth century, especially German, Italian, and English.[12] The influence of British Constitutionalism, the massive invasion of German historicism in various forms, the discovery of Vico—these and other impulses contributed to the upsurge in historical studies; and repercussions could be heard and seen in many fields of culture, especially painting and music. Seldom before and never since (not even in the heyday of late nineteenth-century historical "science," and certainly not in the "new histories" of twentieth-century confection) has historical scholarship had such an international base and intercultural character. Perhaps the most striking illustration of this cosmopolitanism (specifically in connection with the study of law) is in the work of that most nationalistic of all historians, Jules Michelet. Although Michelet has never lost his position as founding father of modern French historical studies, his example in this regard has not often been followed.

For intellectual history broadly conceived, however, it will not do to accept the conceptual limitations inherited from conventional histories of literature or philosophy, which is to say to surrender to the confines of a retrospectively canonized text, even Michelet's or Thierry's. Recent narrativist (or "narratological") studies of historiography have yielded fascinating insights and connections; but certain rhetorical analyses, such as those of Hayden White and Lionel Gossman, nevertheless do aspire to reach beyond the textual world to a social, or shared, "ideology."[13] Without denying the value of this (newest of new) history, I would suggest that it not only accepts but tries to make a virtue of one of the weaknesses of old-fashioned intellectual history, which is to leap directly from a publicly (and often artistically) formulated interpretation to some collective consciousness or intellectual model conceived of in excessively (and perhaps inaccessibly) "internalist" terms. A more comprehensive appreciation of historical scholarship, beyond but including historical narrative, requires attention also to other considerations. Among these I would emphasize the importance of trying to gain familiarity with the wider world of historical discourse beyond privileged literary texts and formally defined disciplines. The study of history is an enterprise carried on in a large arena of discourse, with intrusions from other conversations and fields of interest, with scholarly interchange and criticism, and, last but not least, with input from source materials. If history is not a hard science, we should not forget that at some points it is constrained by an uncaring reality, or at least evidence thereof.

Sometimes, especially when reading Michelet or Thierry, we may tend to forget this last point, but this may arise from another weakness of conventional literary or intellectual history: the overemphasis on strong-willed and strong-opinioned spokesmen at the expense of the less conspicuous collectors and interpreters who are often doing more fundamental research and explanation than the great Authors.[14] From the point of view of historical scholarship, for example, Michelet and Thierry were hardly in the same class with such medievalists as Henri Klimrath or even such jurists as J. M. Pardessus. In general, it is the purpose of this book to look below the level of the "mountaintops" (as Meinecke called the grand figures of historicism, such as Herder and Ranke) and to inquire into the external and internal history of early nineteenth-century historical scholarship as a communal, if not always comradely, undertaking whose purpose was indeed not only to fortify or attack one ideology or another, but to probe into the human past and gain deeper understanding of the human condition.

There are no real heroes in this story, then, although Savigny looms in the background and Michelet makes an appearance in chapter 9 as an eccentric illustration of the convergence between law and history. Nor is there any attempt to rehearse the familiar achievements of Romantic narrative

11

historiography, except as it touches on the legal dimension. Instead the focus is on several interrelated facets of and factors in the historical scholarship of the Restoration and July Monarchies. These include the intellectual background of the "new history" (chapter 2), the postrevolutionary ideological context (chapter 3), the connection with jurisprudence especially as reflected in the Civil Code and its interpretation (chapter 4), the scholarly significance of the legal tradition for the study of history (chapter 5), the impact of Savigny and the historical school (chapter 6) and its chief journal in France, *La Thémis* (chapter 7), a handful of the leading legal historians (chapter 8), and a central conceptual problem (chapter 10) and the social issues (chapter 11) shared by the legal and historical scholarship of that age. The common denominator is the historical "resurrection," in a special sense, that Michelet defined as his lifework. The aim remains to investigate the relationship—reciprocal, ambivalent, productive—between Clio and Themis and their variously motivated devotees.

The "New History" of the Restoration

L'histoire nouvelle. . . . Cette restauration des
castes et des races secondaires n'a pas seulement
une justice rendu à l'humanité, ç'a été aussi une
importante conquête pour l'histoire. . . .
—Sarazin (1835)

"History, that task and aptitude of our age, falls heir, in effect, to all other branches of human culture."[1] So wrote Sainte-
Beuve, devotee as well as critic of history, and during the
second quarter of the nineteenth century this discipline seemed
indeed to be taking over the whole range of human and even
natural sciences, not to speak of literature and the arts. As
Auguste Comte put it, "The present century is characterized
above all by the irrevocable preponderance of history, in philosophy, in politics, and even in poetry."[2] As philosophy had
replaced theology, so now history replaced philosophy as queen
of the sciences, the source not only of enlightenment but of
value and direction. It became the key to human understanding, to social salvation, and perhaps to the transcendent form
of humanity. The potential of history as a religious calling
was to be realized above all by Jules Michelet, who saw man
as his own Maker and history as his handiwork. "Be it my
share in the future . . . ," rhapsodized Michelet in 1846, "to
have named history by a name given by no one before. Thierry
calls it *narration* and M. Guizot analysis. I have called it *resurrection*, and it will retain the name."[3]

The "new history" was itself no complete break with the
past. An interest in history had been preserved in certain sur-
vivals of Enlightenment philosophy, symbolized and perhaps
best expressed in the intellectual testament left by Condorcet
and published posthumously in 1795 as a *Historical Tableau* of

the "progress of the human mind" from antiquity to the eighteenth century. Condorcet's ideal, reminiscent of Voltaire's, was a "philosophical history of peoples"; it was carried on by various latter-day *philosophes*—all of them "prophets of Paris" in their own ways—including Positivists and Eclectics, but above all Ideologues.[4] In the same year that Condorcet's book appeared, the Ideologue Volney proclaimed a "new manner of teaching history," referring in particular to the study of customs and language, in a new course established by the Convention. A generation later, similar goals were professed by his colleague Pierre Daunou, whose course taught from 1819 to 1830 advertised a method that was both "analytical" and "philosophical" and that placed particular emphasis on political economy. Although something of an intellectual fossil, Daunou had some influence on both Michelet, who joined him as an official in the national archives after 1830, and Thierry. Despite their high pedagogical hopes, however, the devotees of Ideology (no less than those of the Positive Philosophy) looked with great suspicion on the actual substance of history, since its "facts" were unfortunately "dead" rather than "living"; and as Destutt de Tracy wrote to Degérando, history was a "tableau" less of progress than of "human folly." In the context of such scientism, the intellectual value of history was negative or at best ancillary. In any case, despite their encyclopedic range, the Ideologues did not (any more than the Positivists) contribute in any significant way to the encounter of Clio and Themis, nor to Michelet's humanist vision of "resurrection."

The truth is that historical consciousness in the nineteenth century could not flourish in the bright light of reason; nor could it find adequate expression through the models of natural science or natural law as generally understood. The presumptions of Enlightenment thought had been challenged by the experience of revolution, and the new historians had also to come to terms with this mind-expanding (when not mind-stopping) phenomenon. In what sense did man "make himself" in the French Revolution? It was hardly an exercise in

rationalism, especially not according to the classic interpretation of Michelet. Rather, it was an upsurge of the "nation,"
and its meaning had ultimately to be sought in social structures and behavior patterns, which implied, among other things,
investigation of legal and institutional records. The first task
of the new history, indeed, was to reconstruct that documentary record reflecting the oppressions and crimes of centuries
that reasonable men had long deplored.

In a sense, historical scholarship was by its very nature
counterrevolutionary. In retrospect, it seemed that Jacobinism, ideological embodiment of revolutionary aims, had looked
only to the future; the past was something to be plundered or
effaced. "History" signified servitude, and so did its monuments; "reason" demanded that it be abolished along with the
monarchy, its laws, and its institutions. So Condorcet, even
as he contemplated the vision of humanity's progress over the
centuries, could demand that the archival remains of the Old
Regime be "enveloped in a common destruction."⁵ That was
in 1792, however, and in the aftermath of revolutionary destruction, cooler heads and colder hearts began to prevail. The
tide of revolutionary vandalism against archival deposits,
symbols, and arsenals of monarchical oppression was turned.
The elderly jurist A. G. Camus was appointed archivist less
than two weeks after that famous night of 4 August 1789,
when feudalism was abolished and most monarchical records
thereby rendered obsolete (though not irrelevant).⁶ Through
Camus' efforts and those of his successors, especially Daunou
and Michelet, the remaining records were centralized and
classified and became, along with other institutions, enterprises and published works, conduits of prerevolutionary
learning, mentality, and sensibility.

There were many such conduits, scholarly and professional, and some will be encountered in later chapters. Perhaps the most important was the practice of jurisprudence
itself, which at all times relied on the resources of the old
legal tradition. This is most explicit in the standard handbook
of the legal profession, *Profession of Advocate*, compiled by the

15

same Camus and appearing in several editions, each augmented and updated, between 1770 and 1832.[7] But it is implicit as well in various scholarly undertakings, especially the editing of Old Regime texts—all of which benefited historians as well as jurists. Napoleon himself, who in his imperial phase began to think of himself less as a revolutionary and more as an inheritor and builder, encouraged such historical efforts and traditions as well as newer enterprises, anthropological, archeological, and antiquarian. In general, with feudalism dead and the Church (as some thought) modernized, the Middle Ages began to appear in a new and softer light. With national unity apparently achieved, history itself could be investigated without fear and loathing.

The most direct impulse to historical studies was counterrevolutionary, however, and (despite the Concordat and neoaristocratic institutions) anti-Bonapartist. Historical and legal scholarship had conceptual if not ideological affinities with the views of Vicomte de Bonald, who, like Burke, elevated wisdom and the inertial forces of society above political and legal rationalism. It found reinforcement, too, in Joseph de Maistre's *Considerations on France* of 1797, which invoked transrational forces, divine as well as national, against revolutionary hubris, and in similar attitudes expressed by the young Chateaubriand that same year in his *Historical Essay on Ancient and Modern Revolutions*. Five years later Chateaubriand celebrated even more enthusiastically the fruitful interconnections between "the genius of Christianity" and the "genius of history."[8] "For the modern historian," he wrote, "the perspective opened by Christianity is the change it has effected in the social order." In 1808 Michaud began to publish his monumental history of the Crusades for "consolation," that ancient counterpart of escapism, while for more serious purposes Claude Fauriel, another old Ideologue, was beginning his massive researches into Frankish and Gallic antiquity. Like Daunou, Fauriel later taught at the Sorbonne and was advisor to the next generation of historical-minded scholars.[9] Camus' aforementioned legal handbook was also licensed by Napoleon, and it appeared with all of its feudal and ecclesiastical apparatus, the only concession to modernity being a new section on economics (*l'économie sociale*). A report made in 1808 by Dacier, head of the national library from 1800, listed a variety of historical works, both modern and ancient, and in German and English as well as French, including those to be continued by order of the imperial government.[10]

Yet on the whole the study of history was still at a low ebb in the Napoleonic period. The Emperor's own interest was utilitarian and self-serving. Instruction in history in the national *Université* ("class of ancient and modern literature") was elementary and uncontaminated by any sort of "ideology" (a term to which Napoleon was the first to give a pejorative twist). In 1803 the Emperor tried to insure this academic purity by suppressing the "class of moral and political sciences" of the Institute of France. In general, the publication of historical works was distinguished more by quantity than by quality. The Ideologue J. M. Degérando's *Comparative History of Systems of Philosophy* (1804) was really an elaboration of Condorcet's *Tableau*.[11] Sismondi had not yet turned from Italian to French history, and no other writer of first rank had appeared. Chateaubriand, hardly a serious scholar, deplored the neglect of history and attributed it to the narrow secularism that still intimidated authors. In fact, Dacier's report contained little besides outmoded work of Old Regime scholars; one conspicuous exception was the work of a foreigner, K. F. Eichhorn, whose study of Germanic law contributed in its own way to the "wars of liberation" against Napoleonic legal and military domination—"the revolt of outraged history," as Lord Acton would call them.[12] To admirers of German "liberty" (and critics of the new "Robespierrism") like Charles de Villers, "Buonaparte" was himself an affront to the process as well as the study of history. This was the view taken also by Villers' friend Mme de Staël, who a few years later described in embarrassing detail the inferiority of French to German scholarship.[13]

De l'Allemagne was a sign of things to come, the beginning of a generation-long publicity campaign. Within twenty years, a profound revolution—or perhaps counterrevolution—was accomplished, a phenomenon "deeper and more serious," as Acton wrote, "than the revival of ancient leaning."[14] A quarter century after Dacier's report, a similar survey of "the progress of historical studies in France" bore witness to this revolution. In this bibliographical guide, published in Strasbourg in 1835, Jean Sarazin was pleased to announce the appearance of a "new history," a broad and up-to-date vision of the human and especially the national past going beyond elitist political and military concerns to a "restoration of inferior classes and races."[15] This was not the first—and it would certainly not be the last—of "new histories." La Popelinière's in the sixteenth century opened up historical investigation to global scale and the whole range of arts and sciences, and that of the eighteenth-century *philosophes* continued this expansion.[16] In a sense, the new history of Restoration France was simply carrying on this humanist and enlightened effort, as Sarazin put it, to "render justice to all humanity." But the social conditions of postrevolutionary Europe afforded both greater opportunities and greater incentives to broaden and deepen the investigation of the historical dimension of the human condition. This is the context of Sainte-Beuve's remark about the popularity and intellectual imperialism of history in the early nineteenth century and the background of Michelet's conception of history as "resurrection."

Michelet was undoubtedly the central figure of the historical "revolution" (as Acton called it) in France, but he was riding the crest of a large wave—several waves, in fact—created by the political and intellectual climate of Restoration France.[17] Perhaps the most fundamental impulse came from foreign sources, especially German, as we shall see, but also Italian (particularly Vico) and English (Walter Scott and the Whig political tradition). There was a significant historiographical movement in France, too, and one of the most striking testimonies to it was the last major book of no less a cosmopolitan than Chateaubriand. His *Historical Studies* of 1831 celebrated Vico, Henry Hallam, Herder, and the German historical school and also the grand tradition of French historiography since the sixteenth century (the "ten historians before Mézeray" publicized by Thierry) and "the modern historical school of France," with its descriptive and philosophical branches.[18] Chateaubriand distrusted the "historical fatalism" exhibited by certain liberal authors, most notably Guizot and Thiers, but recognized the powerful impetus given to the study of the past by Restoration politics and by the recent revolution of 1830. This experience moved the young Michelet even more deeply, and he set about quite self-consciously to assume leadership of the historiographical movement. As archivist and teacher as well as scholar and popular author, he helped to promote the various scientific and social goals of this school. His competitors were middle-aged and drawn in any case to public life, but he did not begrudge them credit. Among his elders he gave particular recognition to a distinguished *pléiade* who had already done their part by laying the literary foundation of the new history.[19] Although of only marginal importance for the encounter between Clio and Themis, these authors set the intellectual and stylistic tone for historical writing and deserve at least brief consideration.

The most brilliant figure in this constellation was unquestionably François Guizot, who, intermittently with his political career, served as professor of history at the University of Paris (1812–1815, 1820–1822, and 1828–1830).[20] Like Michelet, Guizot had debts to German scholarship but even more to English, reflected in his monumental edition of Gibbon (1812) and later in his writings on English history. His somewhat romanticized discussions served as a sort of surrogate for the politically more sensitive subject of Restoration France, with 1830 taken as the French counterpart to 1688. But aside from their "political uses," Guizot's liberal and bourgeois views operated to extend historical investigations to social levels traditionally neglected, especially to the Third Estate, which since Siéyès had been virtually identified with the nation, and to phenomena of class conflict and social, institutional, and legal

19

development. The revolution of 1830, which brought Guizot into the government, seemed to justify his vision of history. In 1833 he tried to give it a documentary base by establishing the Société de l'Histoire de France and by collecting unpublished records and chronicles on the order of the German society that over a decade earlier had begun publication of the *Monumenta Germaniae Historica*, whose own nationalist motto was *Sanctus amor patriae dat animum*. Guizot also appointed Michelet head of the historical section of the national archives in 1832 and on several levels devoted himself to "doing justice" to the French past through the vocation of his age, the study of history.

The other four members of Michelet's *pléiade* were all younger colleagues and protégés of Guizot, all members of the Société de l'Histoire de France and concerned in one way or another with countering the antihistorical spirit that was an unfortunate aspect of the revolutionary legacy.[21] All except Barante were trained as lawyers. Adolphe Thiers was fascinated by political history since the Revolution and, like Guizot, kept his eyes on a political career as well as a literary audience. François Mignet, cofounder with Thiers of the newspaper *Le National* in 1830, was more interested in institutions and produced a distinguished series of works on European, especially Spanish, history since the Reformation, as well as a history of the Revolution. Prosper de Barante's reputation rests primarily on his masterly narrative history of the Dukes of Burgundy and, as with his colleagues, an appreciation of the social dimension of history. "Historical interest inclines toward the history of religion," he wrote, "toward the history of legislation, of science, of opinion, and of art as well as toward scenes set on the field of battle, in city squares, and in the courts of kings."[22] This was a conviction held even more passionately by Augustin Thierry, who named the Swiss historian Sismondi as well as Barante and Guizot to the avantgarde of what he called "a veritable revolution in the manner of writing the history of France."[23]

In a sense, Thierry was the real founder of what he referred to in 1824 as the "new historical school."[24] It was he, in any case, who issued its first manifesto in a series of articles published in the summer of 1820 in the *Courrier français*. Former secretary, collaborator, and "adopted son" of Saint-Simon and disillusioned political journalist, Thierry turned away from the public arena more deliberately than his colleagues did and embraced history as both surrogate politics and higher vocation. He pointed in retrospect to his reading of Hume's history in 1817 as the inspiration for his first choice of subject, the Norman conquest, and more generally to his discovery seven years earlier of Chateaubriand's *The Martyrs* for his medievalist interests. Thierry's ambitious and competitive championship of the "new criticism" in historical scholarship was pursued during the 1820s and 1830s in a stream of articles, historiographical and methodological as well as polemical and partisan. Surveying the grand tradition of national historians going back to the pioneering study of institutional history by the sixteenth-century "father" of French historiography, Bernard Du Haillan, Thierry pictured himself as the herald of the second—now historiographical—French Revolution. "Reform of the study of history," he wrote, "reform of the way history is written, war on the writers without learning who failed to see, and on the writers without imagination who failed to depict . . . ; war on the most acclaimed writers of the philosophical school, because of their calculated dryness and their disdainful ignorance of our national origins."[25] Thierry continued the campaign while his four colleagues shifted to political journalism and to more active roles, especially after 1830. In 1836, when Guizot assigned him the task of collecting the sources for a history of the Third Estate, Thierry was able to begin practicing what he had preached about the national— the social and institutional—dimensions of the new history.

If Michelet was the idealist poet of the national soul, Thierry was the enthusiastic antiquarian of "bourgeois liberty." Having celebrated this theme in an English context, he turned to "the formation and progress of the Third Estate" in France. His introductory essay to his documentary survey constituted

21

a sort of institutional hagiography, focusing in particular on the rise of the communes, the Estates General, and the Parlement of Paris, whose "historical destiny" it was to be the conveyors of the aforesaid liberties. The middle class (*la Roture*) had emerged with a cry for equality—"We are men like yourselves," Thierry quoted from the *Roman de la Rose*—and from the twelfth century "renaissance of municipal liberties," it had progressed through a series of "social revolutions," from the "bourgeois revolution" of Etienne Marcel to the eminence perceived by the Abbé Siéyès, which was identification with the "nation" as a whole.[26] In the course of this learned paean to the fundamental "revolutionary movement" of modern history, Thierry emphasized the contributions of the royal legists, historians such as Claude de Seyssel and François Hotman and the seventeenth-century devotees of natural law, who were the real creators of "modern liberal thought," precursors, as it were, of Guizot and the other men (many of them also lawyers) of 1830. Groundbreaking as it was, Thierry's learned work is also as clear an illustration as one can find of that "Whig fallacy" exposed years ago by Herbert Butterfield—in this case, the putative pedigree of the "bourgeois monarchy." But then this was a necessary premise of the new history of the Restoration.

By the 1840s, Michelet had outshone all the members of this *pléiade* (a veritable nova in the firmament of French historical writing), and perhaps the main reason for this was the "eclecticism" that Thierry lamented. Rivalling Guizot in cultural breadth, Mignet in scholarly thoroughness, and Barante in narrative power, Michelet at the same time went further than Thierry in the effort to find new dimensions of social and popular history and deeper than any through his growing familiarity with the national archives.[27] To these qualities, moreover, he added a philosophical, or perhaps metahistorical, dimension that gave direction and meaning to his labors of historical reconstruction—and that made him a target for more orthodox historical critics. For Michelet the great historical epiphany was the "new science" of Vico, and this conception was reinforced by his contacts with German scholarship, including the so-called historical school of law and Creuzer's "symbolic" and Grimm's "poetic" efforts at finding the specific ways in which humanity created itself. These foreign enticements and the interest in legal history Michelet shared with many scholars of his generation. Seldom before or since has French scholarship shown such international breadth of interest and knowledge as in the second quarter of the nineteenth century.

What is the explanation for this cultural epiphenomenon, the resurgence of historical studies after 1815? On the most general level one tendency has been to invoke the many-valued spirit of Romanticism, with all of its fears, hopes, and dreams, its tastes and distastes. Most simplistically, if the Enlightenment was "the fault of Voltaire," Romanticism might with equal validity be blamed (as Irving Babbitt blamed it) on Rousseau. Perhaps, in Baconian terms, it was a victory of "imagination" over both reason and experience, so that art became the model for life. "History is a novel," wrote Alfred de Vigny, "and the People are its author."[28] For many interpreters (and not only Marxists like Lukács) Romanticism has contributed to the "destruction of reason," and history might well be charged as an accomplice.

This is of course to take a very narrow view of "reason." What nineteenth-century devotees of history hoped to do (as did Hegel in his more idealistic way) was to transcend and to subsume what they judged to be the static and shallow rationalism of the previous century. Reactions against such rationalism, whether on grounds of religion, tradition, or instinctual wisdom, produced challenges to "classicism" in a number of guises: classical science, classical literature and art, classical economics, and classical political theory were all called into question. In general, the shift seemed to be from mechanical to biological models in natural science; from abstract formalism to imaginative self-expression in aesthetics; from natural-law cosmopolitanism to national traditions in political theory; from Tracy's Ideology to Victor Cousin's Eclecticism in philosophy.[29] In this alteration of intellectual climate, the French Revolution was a primary agent, not only by awakening national sentiment but also by drawing attention to the crucial question of social change and by itself evolving in the interpretations of later scholarship.[30] The aversion to catastrophe that it inspired, along with an obverse inclination to developmental views even on the part of its later champions, was expressed in fields as disparate as astronomy and geology on the one hand and legislation and international diplomacy on the other. "Historicism" is the word usually associated with this condition of mind, and it certainly is an attitude evident in the work of Michelet, his *pléiade*, and most of his contemporaries.[31]

Yet like Romanticism, "historicism" explains too much; it represents the question, not the answer. Another suggestion has been the attribution of the revival of history to various postrevolutionary ideologies, and again there is some appearance of truth. There is no doubt that the Revolution, together with its imperial aftermath, provokes a wide range of partisan attempts to reexamine the past—both the immediate past as the locus of plans to be continued, problems to be solved, or evils to be resisted, and the more remote past as the source of a deeper understanding of the human predicament in modern times. Resentment, pessimism, and nostalgia were some of the emotions underlying the conservative view of history, which sought to restore religion, authority, order, perhaps a social hierarchy, and certainly institutional continuity with the past. De Maistre, for example, celebrated the ancient constitution, Chateaubriand preached Christian tradition, and Ballanche (from his own eccentric reading of Vico) invoked the "great chain of being" as the foundations of this historical restoration.[32] Liberals shared the sense of continuity, but with a different provenance and a different direction. Guizot revealed the laws of material and cultural progress, a sort of controlled permanent revolution given institutional form through Anglomorphic English constitutionalism and, though bourgeois in origin, eventually encompassing the whole nation, indeed all

of humanity. His version of history became virtually the ideology of the July Monarchy, and in 1830 was given its own
agrégation examination to ensure its orthodoxy.[33] Socialist visions likewise had recourse to history, in a sense combining
conservative yearnings for social order with liberal ambitions
to extend the revolution. Proudhon, for example, saw in the
process of history since antiquity the fundamental dynamic of
the social process, which was class conflict over the possession
of wealth. He also found in it suggestions for the remedy of
social problems, which was a restoration of primitive communal patterns in the context, to be sure, of an industrializing
society.

But these ideological explanations are also unsatisfactory for
the larger epiphenomenon designated by historicism, for obviously the political and social uses of history were demon-
strated by all parties. In fact, history was a mode of perception, conception, and formulation common to many disciplines,
coteries, and interest groups. There is one characteristic that
not only binds together ideological extremes but also seems
essential to the "new history" that emerged in Restoration
France. This was the endless fascination with the "social"—
with social questions and above all the Social Question. Before the Revolution, the focus was on political authority and
political liberty; a generation later, interest had shifted mark-
edly from such abstractions to more practical problems of society, especially property relations. Revolutionary legislation
and the Napoleonic Code were reversed or modified; the social engineering of Jacobins and Bonapartists alike were looked
on with suspicion as means of controlling or directing social
change; and publicists in many ways turned their attentions
from constitutions to institutions, from rulers to "the people."
In this apotheosis of the "social," historical scholarship tended
to follow suit, and sometimes to take the lead.

These were some of the cultural conditions of the extraordinary upsurge of interest in jurisprudence in Restoration
France. This brings us finally to the unprecedented concentration of effort in the field of legal (and by association, insti-

25

tutional and social) history in this same period. Clio and Themis, the muse of history and the goddess of justice, were each exalted by the Romantic imagination, but in conjunction they seem to epitomize the quality as well as one of the scholarly bases of Romantic historicism. More than literature, law was, in Bonald's phrase, "the expression of society."[34] More than language or philosophy or certainly politics, the law provided both form and content—both the means of interpreting and the source material—for the reconstruction of social and cultural history.

The relationship between law and history has of course been abiding: sometimes fruitful, sometimes serendipitous, sometimes downright internecine, but always provocative.[35] For though it is often forgotten, jurisprudence represents a compressed and systematized version, virtually a synchronic counterpart, of a certain dimension of the diachronic human record that is history. Although divergent in methods and aims, jurisprudence, like history, reflects national memory and mythology, tries to make intelligible social behavior and ideals, gives shape and substance to cultural tradition, and assumes a didactic and sometimes official function. What is more, jurisprudence had always claimed to be a human—in professional terms a "legal" or "civil"—science, in particular and often pejorative contrast with natural science. This was also a recommendation for many historians. In 1885 Alfred Jourdan could still write, "The law is social philosophy *par excellence*,"[36] and practitioners of the new history tended also to work from this premise.

Never was the relationship between Clio and Themis warmer than in the early nineteenth century. The warmth derived first from philosophic friction (a conflict inherited from the previous century) and later from intense scholarly and conceptual collaboration. It does not seem possible to appreciate the scope and depth of the "new history" of this period without attending to the circumstances of this union, temporary and tempestuous as it was. Michelet, especially through the influence of Vico and Grimm, was deeply indebted to legal scholarship; so were Thierry, Guizot, and even old Chateaubriand. But there were other offspring of this union of law and history that, although generally overshadowed by the popularity of Michelet and his *pléiade*, were perhaps more self-conscious and certainly no less important for historical scholarship and interpretation. Some of these lost souls may deserve their obscurity—academic and legal careerists, wrangling and partisan pedants, visionless dry-as-dusts, overeducated pettifoggers, illiberal defenders of the status quo, as many of them seem—but others, at least enough to challenge the celebrated *pléiade*, deserve notice on intellectual as well as scholarly grounds.[37] They too illustrated "that task and aptitude of our age" pointed out by Sainte-Beuve; they too contributed to that new history advertised by Chateaubriand, Thierry, and Sarazin and to the efforts of "resurrection" headed by Michelet. Standing among the founders of that "scientific history" usually discussed in the context of the late nineteenth century, they form a missing chapter in the history of historical scholarship. This minor effort of "resurrection" is one of the purposes of the following inquiry.

CHAPTER THREE

In the Wake of Revolution

Je n'aime pas à parler des vaincus.
—Guizot (1820)

The "new history" was obsessed with European antiquity but could not escape the pressure of the most recent past. The French Revolution had been all things to all men—especially French men. An end and a beginning, a sharp "break with the past" (in Thierry's words), a culminating phase of history (according to Tocqueville), another face of Romanticism (Victor Hugo decided), the birth of the nation (urged Michelet), the start of a great liberation (liberals were confident), and the source of great injustice (lamented royalists). In any case, the Revolution produced an enormous mythology. In the following generations every public figure in France, as well as most literary figures, found political and social identity in the ideological terms of the political spectrum defined, indeed calibrated, by the seating arrangements of the revolutionary assemblies.[1] From right to left and back to right, from monarchy to republic (and more radical forms) and back to empire, this trajectory has defined political positioning behavior and legitimation ever since the killing of the king. Neither counterrevolution nor Bonapartism nor Restoration has changed this metric scale of politics, however misleading it may seem in retrospect. The need to sort out and make sense of these positions, thereby placing the revolutionary experience in political perspective, furnished perhaps the most immediate motive for historical study. This is one reason history was so central to nineteenth-century thought and action.

There were other reasons not tied directly to politics. They derived most often from weariness of, or hostility toward, the rationalist hubris of the "philosophical school" of the Enlightenment, in reference mainly to Rousseau and Voltaire, if not Montesquieu.[2] Before 1789, evolutionist theories were already invading the natural sciences (astronomy as well as biology), human studies (history, law, philosophy, and literature), and even divinity (theology and Biblical exegesis). Political thought and political economy, too, increasingly accommodated ideas of historical change, whether conceived in terms of Burkean conservatism, Fichtean national development, liberal "progress," or indeed more radical or utopian social transformation. Most directly, these attitudes were manifested in the rise of a series of so-called historical schools of law, economics, and language and literature—and of course in a dramatic upsurge in historical scholarship itself.[3] What revolutionary and Bonapartist ideology did was establish a focus and target for the attitudes of unfocused and perhaps aimless historicism. What the Restoration did was create a suitable climate of opinion (if not an institutional base) for such views. What the revolution of 1830 did was provide further impetus for a social dimension and (to enthusiasts like Guizot) a *terminus ad quem* for historical interpretation.

"Historicism" of course had deeper roots, going back into some of the less celebrated levels of Enlightenment thought, back to even earlier traditions of philology and social philosophy; but opposition to the Revolution furnished fertile soil for growth and eventual flowering in modern forms. One *locus classicus* was fixed by Edmund Burke, who seized almost immediately on the fallacies of what came to be called "Jacobinism," and whose *Reflections* circulated at least five French editions during the first two years of the Revolution. For Burke the French Revolution represented the absolute perversion of true "liberty" and "constitution," both of which, he protested, were the products not of overnight construction, or destruction, but of long and unreflective development. The "nature" perceived by Burke was a product of normal growth rather than artificial reason, and legitimacy was acquired most fundamentally by prescription rather than legislation. English

29

prejudice against "hurrying enlighteners," in Coleridge's phrase, was intensified by the influence of Continental Romanticism and contributed to modern conservatism.

A similar position was taken by celebrators of German nationality like J. G. Herder, who made social instinct, or *Volksgeist*, the basic category of history, and Fichte, who took a more elevated and political view of national tradition. The divergent and in a sense populist construction of "enlightenment" offered by German authors had already begun to temper the more elitist views of the French when Mme de Staël celebrated the virtues of German civilization.[4] The German wars of liberation against Napoleon intensified appreciation for traditional and sometimes imperceptible structures and values; and it was the intention of the Congress of Vienna, among other things, to repair the damage done by Bonapartist imperialism by restoring an order that drew its legitimacy from history rather than from pure reason. International diplomacy, too, became Burkean (if not Fichtean) in style, though problems of nationality and unfinished "revolution" remained. From the point of view of scholarship, the dilemma of 1815 may be seen in effect as a conflict between right-wing and left-wing historicism—the nineteenth-century version of social theory based on equilibrium versus that based on conflict.

In France, too, there was a fundamental conflict between legitimacy and nationality. In historical terms, the difficulty was that the French had too many "pasts," each claimed by at least one faction. Embittered émigrés and frustrated Bonapartists, cryptofeudal royalists and constitutional royalists, monarchist liberals and republic liberals, and a pandemonium of "social," and soon "socialist," reformers ranging from Christian revivalists to revolutionary Carbonari—all invoked history as a means of justification and prophecy. Partisan constructions of history of course varied widely, from the antiquarian hopes of returning émigrés, who planned to restore as much of the status quo ante as possible, to the equally selective memories of others, victims and beneficiaries alike, who looked to acquire, reacquire, or preserve what they re-

garded as their due, to the revolutionary dispossessed and
malcontents who dreamed of turning revolutionary or counterrevolutionary energies into different channels. Liberals,
Ultras, Theocrats, Ideologues, Doctrinaires, Independents,
Eclectics, Babouvists, Saint-Simonians, Carbonari, and hosts
of fellow-travelers rested and defended their programs on particular views or visions of history, and above all on the proper
meanings of "revolution" and "restoration."

The Restoration yearned for legitimacy, and so did the various parties and social groups trying to find a place in the new
"world restored." The Revolution and Empire had called into
question not just the monarchy and its values but virtually
every institution of French society, including the family and
domestic relations, property, and inheritance. Social continuity was broken, at least in terms of public opinion, and the
premises of law and legitimacy had been divorced from the
processes of history. How could people reconcile their new
predicament with old values? How could they, once again,
join the real with the ideal? This dual problem of understanding and legitimation, of gaining a valid perspective on the past
and finding a justification for the present, is another way of
stating my central theme, the convergence between history
and law.

The political side of the story is quite familiar. The Charter
was granted to the French people by Louis XVIII "in the
nineteenth year of his reign" as if returning history to its old
channels, and the superficial analogy with British constitutionalism made the interpretation plausible. There were historical, political, and social factors, however, that made such
an institutional suture impossible: carry-overs from the Empire, especially the Civil Code and centralized administration
and education; the failure to follow Montesquieu's advice about
the separation of powers; and the unbridgeable divisions between the losers (émigrés and Bonapartists), winners (as Guizot thought of his "middle class"),[5] and those not even admitted to the game. The Charter could affirm the principles of
representative government, civil and religious liberty, free-

31

dom of the press, and the sanctity of property; but the realities of class division and ideological discord, reflected so vividly in the White Terror and Carbonarist conspiracies, made such formulas empty legalisms. Despite invocations of social order and national unity, what emerged after 1815 and especially after 1820 was not a Burkean "constitution" but the clamor and struggle of "parties" (most offensive epithet of Old Regime political philosophy), unrestrained by a regular elective process or legislative safeguards, and dependent in any case on the crown. The Ultras, inspired by Chateaubriand but better exemplified by Bonald, opposed the charter as a basis of "restoration"; the Independents, emerging in the wake of the 1817 elections, inclined on the other hand to reject the monarchy, at least surreptitiously. This left the center, a jumble of constitutional monarchists, a self-proclaimed "party of movement" under the misnamed leadership of the Doctrinaires, that could by no means, except for a brief period before 1820, provide a base for stable government. No wonder Guizot made the parallel with the English restoration after Cromwell—and dreamed of 1688.

In the midst of such political pandemonium, the realities of the historical process and the ideals of jurisprudence seemed irreconcilable. The widening divergence of right and left and the collapse of the middle became irreversible from 1820, when the external threat of revolution, the assassination of the Duke of Berry, and elections weighted by the law of the "double vote" toward the landed proprietors prepared the way for the increasingly reactionary government under Villèle, especially after the succession of Charles X in 1824. The garish ceremony of anointing (the *sacre*) after the coronation in May 1825, which was attended not only by Chateaubriand and Lamartine but also by Victor Hugo and Charles Nodier (newly appointed librarian of the Arsenal and, until his withdrawal, official historiographer of the crowning), illustrated the antiquarian religiosity and, some thought, ultramontane leanings of royalism.[6] Reactions ranged from Hugo's deferential ode to Bérenger's sarcastic lyric on "Charles the Simple," which ridiculed the pseudomiraculous releasing of birds in the cathedral of Rheims (a practice unknown to the Old Regime) but added that at least *they* were free. Behind the spuriously historical symbolism of this nostalgic royalism lurked more direct counterrevolutionary threats, most notably the notorious Law of Sacrilege, which was voted by the Chamber just a month earlier. But neither ultramontanism nor old-fashioned Gallicanism (modernized by Napoleon's Concordat) could restore its traditions. Religion and ecclesiology, too, had to come to terms with the Revolution and with history, but that is another story.

During the Restoration (as in the Revolution) social and economic problems were pivotal. More directly related to the law than to political squabbling and (as secular-minded Ultras, liberals, and "socialists" alike would agree) historically more fundamental was the great question left unanswered through the first quarter of the nineteenth century: the possession of land taken over and still in dispute in the wake of the Revolution and its various confiscations. Returning émigrés certainly wanted to recover lost properties if not restore *la féodalité* in more general terms, as some journalists charged. To this end they initiated endless lawsuits and, according to one authority, violent usurpation and duels to the death.[7] Curiously and ironically, "old" and "new proprietors," usually noble and bourgeois respectively, seemed to have exchanged theories of law and history, the former claiming the "absolute" right of property against revolutionary "usurpation" and the latter appealing to prescription and possessory rights. Ensuing debates, crucial to both law and history, were inflammatory, interminable, and in more than one sense groundbreaking. Indemnification seemed the only solution to the dilemma. The Civil Code demanded it (*prélable* was the operative term), but the question remained: Who was to receive and to whom was "due" the indemnity, the *ancien* or the *nouveau propriétaire*?[8] Like the political controversy, this early version of the Social Question seemed to admit of no reasonable—or even historical—compromise. In fact the Law of

33

Indemnity, also of 1825, pleased no party. On this most fundamental issue there was no way to render justice, to repair damage done by the "break with the past," but there was massive incentive to inquire into one of the most basic problems of legal and social history.

The most spectacular of the conflicts in the Restoration came over, as well as in, the press; and it was perhaps the first time that a major medium came to overshadow the messages of controversy. "The journal and the book are the two organs of modern thought; the ancients knew only the oration and the manuscript," wrote Eugène Lerminier, one of the most successful exploiters of the print medium in the second quarter of the century.[9] And not only of modern thought, he might have added from his own experience, but also of modern political and social action. This threat the government authorities well understood, and they responded in the same way that Napoleon and indeed Old Regime authorities had done. After 1820 the principle of freedom of the press was largely a dead letter, and official intimidation of journalism was reinforced by "caution money" as well as by censorship. This policy affected scholarly and professional publication as well as political journalism, for one of the characteristics of the remarkable upsurge of periodicals in the Restoration was its encyclopedic and interdisciplinary range. Right, center, and (especially) left journals of the 1820s conscripted the best talents in all fields, and historians were in the vanguard. All the members of Michelet's *pléiade* (Guizot, Thiers, Mignet, Barante, and Thierry) contributed scholarly and polemical articles to the major journals, including the *Journal des débats*, the *Constitutionnel*, the *Revue encyclopédique*, the *Courrier français*, the *Revue française*, and especially the *Globe*. Behind these were the more specialized professional journals, such as the *Gazette des tribunaux* and *La Thémis*, whose covert but significant role has gone more or less unappreciated in the mass of literature on Restoration journalism.[10]

These journals and others like them, often short-lived and sometimes forcibly or fiscally suppressed, constituted a battleground where party lines were drawn and wars fought over matters historical, literary, and artistic as well as legal, social, and political. They constituted also the planting ground for Romanticism and other unsettling cultural movements tied to the broader enterprise of evaluating (or revaluing) the cultural past of France, most notably medieval and Renaissance sources of inspiration. They constituted, too, a haven for a truly "eclectic" variety of foreign influences: the mania for Shakespeare and Scott, the fascination with Dante and Vico, and especially the boundless interest in things Germanic, from Herder to Hegel. Journals like the *Globe* represented the headquarters of "young France" (the phrase was coined by one of the *Globe's* founders, Pierre Dubois) and of the "young university," as Charles de Rémusat called Guizot, Thiers, and other academic exiles hoping to publish their way into political activism and public life. Rémusat recalled the many discussions in Parisian cafés carried on by members of this "*Globe* brigade," which included Thiers, Mignet, Cousin, and J. J. Ampère, the literary historian. To at least one such gathering, a dinner at Fauriel's house, the archfatalist Hegel himself came. "It was out of this milieu that emerged the doctrine of historical fatalism," Rémusat remarked, an idea carried at times to the point of "absurd exaggeration and dangerous inflexibility."[11] Thierry, Sainte-Beuve, and others were on at least the periphery of this circle, and so eventually was Michelet.

Behind the historical dogmatizing recalled by Rémusat and later criticized by Chateaubriand and Michelet, more subversive thoughts were brewing. The journalism of the 1820s was engaged both in a scholarly assault on French cultural tradition and, increasingly boldly, in opposition to the government of Villèle and especially Polignac (who truly wanted, it seemed, to turn the clock back). These two campaigns overlapped. Even more pointed than the thrusts of the *Globe* were the attacks of *Le Temps*, a new journal founded by Guizot in the fall of 1829. Michelet published in *Le Temps* a review of the new translation of Niebuhr's Roman history in June 1830 and one of a new book by his friend Edgar Quinet that October.[12] In the mean-

35

time, the journal had played an active role in the July revolution, which replaced Charles X with Louis-Philippe, brought
Guizot to power, and, incidentally, gave Michelet a liberal
vision of history that confirmed his life-calling as national historian.

The "three glorious days" of July 1830 have been characterized as a "bourgeois revolution," and, head-counting aside,
the judgment seems appropriate in terms of the perceptions
and intentions of the leading participants.[13] "I said to myself,"
wrote Heinrich Heine, "Germany *can* be free."[14] It is true of
course that below the political level there was little change
beyond widening the social base of the Chamber of Deputies
through suffrage reform. The lower bourgeoisie was already,
despite indemnification, in decline. But 1830 certainly inclined to the benefit of property-owners, whatever their class
provenance. Society seemed in any case to be dominated by
the "mythology" or "cult of the ego" (*culte du Moi*), as one
critic put it, both in leadership and in scholarship (sometimes
in the same person, as with Guizot).[15] The tone was set by
what Saint-Marc Girardin called the "bourgeois aristocracy,"
which included journalists and jurists as well as commercial
and financial personages.[16]

The July days have also been referred to as a "revolution
of the advocates," and there was something in this, too.[17] Corresponding to the bourgeois aristocracy was virtually a rein-
carnation of the old "parlementary nobility."[18] Except for their
costume, the *hommes de loi* and the *propriétaires* seemed inter-
changeable, especially in their vices—recall the vitriolic caricatures of Daumier.[19] "The magistracy," wrote its modern
historian, "arose to power with the bourgeoisie from which it
came," especially in the August "insurrection of office-seek-
ers."[20] Naturally, there was a substantial turnover in the royal
courts (13 of 27), but the crucial Cour de Cassation was left
untouched, and the percentage of lawyers elected in the new
Chamber of Deputies tripled. The most renowned jurist (and
bâtonnier of the Order of Advocates), André Dupin, was counsel for the opposition paper, *Le Constitutionnel*, and a leading

2. *Gens de justice* in the July Monarchy, by Daumier.

participant in the July days. As a recent historian has re-marked, the lawyers were never on the losing side. During the July days, when the *Globe* decided to publish in the face of government prohibitions, Dupin refused to allow his client to cooperate. "Don't forget you are in the office of a lawyer," he warned when the suggestion was made; and while leaving, Pierre Leroux, the other founder of the *Globe* (and coiner of the term *solidarité*), sighed to Rémusat, "Ah, the lawyers, the lawyers!"[21]

Without being too facetious it might almost be suggested that the July days constituted a revolution also of the histori-ans. Certainly the most distinguished of these, Guizot, was more forceful than the most distinguished jurist, Dupin. Though trained as a lawyer, Guizot spoke as a historian when he reflected, unabashedly, that he had "had the honor of car-rying the flag of the middle classes, which was naturally my own."[22] "Our minds were full of the English revolution of 1688," he recalled; and along with such colleagues as Thiers, Mignet, and Barante, he played a significant role in the polit-ical transformation of 1830. From writing history these men turned to making it, or at least, as Thiers later told Charles X, to catching one of its larger waves. And at least for a time, they believed they had truly grasped the nature of the histor-ical process, that they were bringing about the reconciliation of the reality of history and the ideality of law.

The impact of the July days on historians ranged from dis-may to exhilaration. "I was writing ancient history when modern history knocked on my door," said Chateaubriand. "In vain I called, 'Wait, I'm coming.' She passed on and took with her three dynasties of kings."[23] With Michelet it was very different. "I commenced to exist, that is, to write, at the end of 1830," he recalled.[24] He was ready to take over lead-ership of that "new history" that Chateaubriand was celebrat-ing when he was so rudely interrupted. If to historians like Guizot 1830 seemed the very culmination of history, to those like Louis Blanc it was a sham. Still, it did focus attention, even antiquarian attention, upon what was to right and left alike the central question of the age: the nature of property. The dominance of historicism insured that this question would be posed as the *origin* of property and so would further encourage the convergence of law and history.

In retrospect the July Monarchy was a bitter disappointment to all parties. "The bourgeois of France is possessed by the demon of destruction," concluded Heine.[25] Journalism continued to expand, to protest, and of course to be repressed. The *Globe* moved leftward to Saint-Simonianism, while its cultural role was taken up by the most "encyclopedic" of all journals, the *Revue des deux mondes*, which was enhanced in its early years by the articles of Michelet, Sainte-Beuve, Lerminier, Rossi, and others who figure in later chapters.[26] But "revolution" had brought France no closer to justice, and history seemed to have provided no answers to the questions left in the wake of the great Revolution. Romantic nostalgia turned to Bonapartism or to republicanism, though of course the "nation" continued to be invoked as unerring and ultimately triumphant. Radicalism broke into a bewildering and increasingly contradictory variety of panaceas and prophecies, from Positivism to utopian solidarism, to old- and new-fashioned ideas of revolution. All lawyers like Dupin cared about, it seemed to such critics as Blanc and Daumier, were their places and their fees.[27] Guizot's old "party of movement" had become an elite club declining into stasis and corruption, increasingly incapable of adapting to more recent challenges of the historical process. If Guizot, arguably the greatest French historian of the postrevolutionary generation, could not learn from history, who could? (Nobody could, decided Tocqueville during the next generation, but that was after the experiences of 1848.)

There was a missing element in Guizot's understanding of history, and indeed in that of most of his contemporaries, including the "new historians." They seem to have lacked a sufficient appreciation of the social dimension of the historical process, and it was precisely what the experiences of 1830 brought to the forefront of French public, or at least intellectual, opinion. It was just at this juncture that the concept and terminology of the "social" (usually in contrast with the pejorative "political" or "economic") was becoming not only fashionable but irresistible.[28] The word "social" found new associations: *liberté sociale, économie sociale, physiologie sociale, organisation sociale, mathématiques sociaux, industrie sociale,* and above all *science sociale.* The term was in everyone's mouth in the early nineteenth century, and soon also were its various offspring, including "sociology" and "socialism." Nor to begin with was there any particular derogatory connotation; even Metternich could call himself a "socialist."

Ideological divergences would come later. What this linguistic phenomenon signified in general was a shift of focus from problems of political and constitutional organization to the structure and tensions of society, intensified by proprietary, financial, and industrial forces that were deepening class divisions. Complicating matters was that old bourgeois totem and justification for proprietary hegemony, "labor" (and in that sense "industry"), which increasingly took an abstract and "social" form, and so became alienated from its human agency. Whence the endlessly debated problems of class division, so central to both the "bourgeois monarchy" and the "new history" of this period. It is in this ideological context that the convergence between history and law, *locus classicus* of the "social," is to be understood. Behind "scientific questions" lurked always the Social Question.

CHAPTER FOUR

History and the Civil Code

Mon Code est perdu!
—Napoleon

Clio was only a muse, but Themis, the title of more than one
nineteenth-century work devoted to legal reform, was wife of
Jupiter and goddess of social order. She was "the force that
brings and binds men together" and the personification of the
science of law.[1] Before 1848, jurisprudence was still the major
vehicle of thought and action about society, though it was in
the process of being superseded by its upstart offshoots, political (or "social") economy, sociology, and then anthropology.[2] In the post-Napoleonic age, however, the study of law
noticeably increased in prestige and was reinforced by the
general shift of attention from political and constitutional to
social and economic questions. This was the case even with
many who maintained a revolutionary faith. "Is it necessary
to make a political or a social revolution?" was a question
posed by members of a younger generation in the 1830s, according to C. G. Hello, a commentator on "the philosophy of
history of France" and jurist who was trying to close the generational gap. "It is necessary to make a social revolution," he
responded—adding, however, that it was advisable to carry
this out through modern "social science," which was the product above all of legal and historical wisdom.[3]

In France, as almost everyone assumed, the political revolution was over; what remained was for various social groups
to accommodate themselves to it, to consolidate and further
it, or to resist it (but on the whole by legal means). Even the
July days were a legalistic sort of coup, and the conspirators
of the *Charbonnerie* played no significant part in the events. In

41

general, the agencies of preservation or modification seemed to be laws and institutions, often with encouragement from the press. The aim of all but the most eccentric public observers was not to redirect the course of history (there had been enough of that since 1789), but only to control or benefit from its flow, to transform perhaps the texture and even leadership but not the structure of society. This tended to be the premise of liberals and early "socialists" as well as conservatives and all but the most desperate malcontents, left or right, at least until the 1840s. In short, across the political spectrum intellectuals were coming to terms with history and looking for its social as well as its "political" uses.[4] And as the experts in the latter search were the Ideologues, journalists, Doctrinaires, and would-be politicians like Guizot and Thiers, so the authorities in matters of social change were the servants of Themis, the jurists. If the influence of the latter was less conspicuous, it was no less effective and certainly more enduring despite the political disturbances of 1830 and 1848.

Clearly, the legalistic approach to "social science" was very much at odds with the ideological presumptions of the previous generation, with all of its faith in natural law and hopes for radical national change, whether Bonapartist or Jacobin. It was certainly at odds with modern theories of codification, such as the utilitarian approach of Bentham. And it was especially at odds with that centerpiece of revolutionary legislation, the Code Civil (né Napoléon), which despite its libertarian rhetoric was by design an almost totalitarian effort of social control.[5] The Code was at once an assault on and a monument to history. In some ways, though, it was an imitation monument; for Napoleon patterned his career on the Roman emperors, especially Justinian, in both his military plans and his legislative ambitions (arma cedunt togae). Like Justinian, Napoleon abolished the republican institution of the consulate, posed as a classical hero, and assumed a transcendent mission to master not only the world but also imperial society, from top to bottom. Like the Corpus Juris Justiniani, the Civil Code was intended to be a perfect and permanent counterpart to the imperial political structure, a construction that "should fix forever the empire of liberty and the destinies of France."[6] This imperial hubris constituted a challenge to historians, who were only too aware of the disparity between legal ideals and social reality, and to jurists, whose business it was to adapt the one to the other.

Roman imperial legislation and Napoleon's Romanoid adaptation of 1804 represented a prototype of what has come to be called social engineering. It was the ideal of enlightened despotism and, more radically, of Jacobinism. ("Do you want good laws?" Voltaire had asked. "Burn your own and make new ones.")[7] It was also the epitome of Bonapartism and persisted into the Restoration, still in the image of the benevolent law-giver. As imperial artists romanticized Napoleon's lawmaking postures, so Delacroix depicted a heroic Justinian reading his legal corpus in a painting (now unfortunately lost) commissioned by the Conseil d'Etat in 1826.[8] Above all, legislation was an expression of the sovereign will and thus, for Jacobins and for Napoleon, the General Will. During the discussions by the redactors of the Code, most of which were attended by the First Consul, it was proposed that for practical reasons there be a delay of two weeks between promulgation and enforcement, but Napoleon objected on the grounds that this "would be an offense to the national will."[9] So he ordered revisions based on calculations of the time necessary for the communication of legislative commands to the provinces, a delay of one day for every twenty leagues after Paris on the first of the month and the department of the Seine on the third. Thus the imperial will would emanate mathematically, concentrically, and inexorably from its legislative source and reflect back on its national foundation. Few questioned the principle of *la volonté générale*. The main question was: How was this force to be expressed, explained, and applied?

The crux of the matter was the age-old legal problem of "interpretation," which was the professional way of expressing the continuing rivalry, in the terms made famous by Montesquieu, between the legislature and the judiciary. Both Justinian and Napoleon had tried legislatively to prohibit lawyers from tampering with their sacred texts, outlawing those commentaries that, as one Bonapartist jurist lamented, "destroy the Code."[10] Napoleon himself expressed the hope "gradually to bring about such a state of affairs that barristers would be quite superfluous."[11] In the preliminary discussions of the Code the very mention of the word "interpretation" caused an uproar; nor were the fears allayed when the Minister of Justice went on to distinguish legislative from (mere) judicial interpretation.[12] Imperial jurists, not only the redactors but also the somewhat sycophantic school of exegesis called "the cult of 1804," would have none of this. Citing the warnings of Montesquieu, the redactor Maillia de Garat protested that all the abuses of the Old Regime could return through the loophole of judicial interpretation. Of course, some interpretation was eventually to Napoleon's benefit, such as the adulatory commentary published in 1809 by J.B.V. Proudhon.[13] But the great "hero" of legal history, as Proudhon referred to the Emperor, well understood (for he too had read his history) that lawyers would not voluntarily keep their hands off the work of the lawmakers and would somehow usurp it: *cujus interpretatio, ejus legislatio*. No wonder Bonaparte, watching the rising tide of jurisprudence, is said to have cried, "My Code is lost!"[14]

And so in the long run, it was. What Montesquieu idealized as a balance between legislature and judiciary could also be seen as a basic dialectic of history, a continual reshaping of established law by the appliers, practitioners, and evaders: Themis under assault by the forces of Clio. Since preserving the letter of their law was impossible even for Bonapartists, it was necessary to have recourse to the "spirit" in the richly evocative term of Montesquieu, and Jean Domat before him, applied by the Baron Locré to his authoritative commentary of 1805.[15] In Roman law this "spirit" meant the original intention of the legislator (*mens legum* was the technical term used by Domat and Vico, and rendered *esprit des lois* by Montesquieu and others), but beyond this it had come to imply the reason or rationality of a particular rule. In this way the door was opened further to the interminable debate ("vain discord of posterity," Justinian had called it) lamented by Napoleon.

The debate, recorded in the "preparatory work of the Code," was essentially between such idealists as Cambacérès, who hoped to "foresee everything" and "regenerate everything," and more practical- and historical-minded jurists who from experience knew better. In 1798 Count Cambacérès had given a "Discourse on Social Science," celebrating the devices of political reason, including the calculations of political economy and especially the art of legislation; and he preserved this utopian stance from the heady days of '93 until publication of the Code over a decade later. He was opposed by Count Portalis in the "Preliminary Discourse to the Code" and by other professional lawyers in their remarks. There had been judges even before there were laws, remarked one redactor. And as for the future, Citizen Portalis rejected his rival Cambacérès' optimism by remarking that "to foresee everything is impossible."[16] If this was true in political terms, how much more did it apply to private law and the intricate web of human relations to which it applied?

Out of this unavoidable juridical process came the interminable interpretations of the academic commentators in Napoleon's newly founded *Université*, and in this tradition Romanist influence was dominant for at least a generation. "This Code," wrote one admirer of Napoleon's masterwork even before its publication, "is founded principally on Roman law."[17] The analogy was evident in both its form ("Romanoid") which followed that of Justinian's *Institutes*, and its substance, most notably in the apparently "bourgeois" but historically Romanist formulations of the law of property and contract. A recent historian of the Code has referred to the "bourgeois peace" of the nineteenth century (the *paix bourgeoise*, analogous to the *pax Romana* of Augustus) and has argued that the rules of this "bourgeois game" of economic competition, acquisition, and mastery were set down in classical form in the Code, just as the social rules for Roman citizens had been set down in classical jurisprudence and finally in Justinian's Corpus Juris.[18] There is a further parallel, for if both codifications were assembled by legal experts under imperial direction, they were also in a deeper sense popular creations. Roman law was established "by the force and grandeur of the Roman people," pleaded Chabot d'Allier in 1819; it was "l'ouvrage du peuple roi," wrote Cotelle not long after this, referring to the famous *lex regia* by which the prince derived his authority from the *populus*.[19] Critics pointed to the delusion common to the Romans and French that they had created a permanent ideal out of the flow of history. "The French who since 1804 imagined that they had salvaged the Revolution because they possessed their five codes," remarked Quinet, "argued like the Byzantines, who also thought that they had preserved Athens and Rome and the heroic soul of ancient civilization, because Justinian had given them the Digests and the Pandects."[20]

Through pedagogical encouragement from such scholars and teachers, Romanist influence did not decline but actually increased, despite the indigenous growth of French jurisprudence. From the short-lived Academy of Legislation and University of Jurisprudence established during what one historian has called a "renaissance of juridical studies" under the Consulate, to their more successful imperial successor, the Ecole de Droit, professors insisted on the utility of Roman theory as a preliminary to French practice.[21] In 1807 Dupin, the law school's first graduate, called for a return to the old Romanist tradition represented by Jacques Cujas.[22] The Restoration did not change this assumption, and similar advice continued to be given, especially at the openings of competitions for professorships in Roman law. In 1828 Ortolan, in 1836 Dupin, and in 1837 Blondeau were still defending Roman law on the grounds that it contained not a static legislation but a dynamic jurisprudence open, as Blondeau put it, to "an interpretation relevant to the spirit of modern times." One reason for this professional affection was that Roman law was a locus of natural law arguments that older-fashioned jurists continued to use. Even more important was the fact that so much professional legal apparatus—methods, arguments, and centuries of precedents and literature—was attached to the Roman tradition. In any case, Roman law and Roman history continued to be essential for the understanding of French institutions, and historians as well as jurists were conditioned in their training by this assumption. French lawyers too were, in the famous Roman formula, "priests of the laws" (*sacerdotes legum; prêtres de la justice*).[23]

What makes the parallel between French and Roman law still more striking is the fact that the career of the Code practically recapitulated that of the Romano-Byzantine corpus after its formation in the sixth century by Justinian, and especially after its revival in the twelfth century and incorporation into the university curriculum. Corresponding to Tribonian and other members of Justinian's editorial committee of 529 was Napoleon's committee of redaction headed by Cambacérès. Corresponding to the thirteenth-century glossators was the so-called exegetic school (*école de l'exégèse*), which also took a narrow-minded construction of the text and tended to make a fetish of the "intention" of the imperial redactors. The *exégètes* more or less avoided recourse to history but had an advantage over the medieval glossators: they had access to a record of the debates of the original editors, assembled authoritatively in the analysis published by Jacques Maleville in 1805.[24] Of the edifice of academic jurisprudence in France, men such as Maleville, the elder Proudhon, Delvincourt, and especially Charles Toullier were the founders if not actually the builders.

Corresponding to the legal scholasticism of Bartolus and his fourteenth-century colleagues who succeeded the glossators was what has been called the "dogmatic school," the "grand commentators" who likewise (and with similar motives) began to rationalize, systematize, and modernize the law for the benefit of contemporary industrializing and capitalizing society. It was partly with this in mind that one member of this school, A. M. Demante, quoted the old civilian maxim that "custom

47

is the best interpreter of law," implying that "interpretation" depended on contemporary social conditions, political interests, and the "will" both of the people (the ultimate source of custom) and of the legislator.[25] Other members of this school include the elder Proudhon, who graduated from the *école de l'exégèse* later to publish two highly apologetic commentaries on private property and on the public domain under the "bourgeois monarchy"; Raymond Troplong, who carried Guizot's liberal doctrines from political historiography into private law; and J. Frédéric Taulier, who had even stronger ties with the new history, commending not only Guizot, Troplong, and Thierry but also Michelet and Vico for their contributions to the deepening of the philosophy of law. Writing after 1830, all of these jurists joined the chorus of praise for the growing *embourgeoisement* of French law and for its alliance with historical scholarship.

Finally, corresponding to what has been called the "first historical school of law" in the sixteenth century there appeared an approach based on historical criticism and interpretation that moved further and further beyond the concerns of the legal profession.[26] The parallel between the Renaissance of the fifteenth century and the revival of studies in the nineteenth century extends also to the field of law. In addition to editions and textual studies, legal scholars devoted themselves to the investigation of a whole series of "pasts," including the "written reason" (*ratio scripta; raison écrite*) of Roman law and the unwritten reason of natural law, the accumulated rules of feudal custom and positive law, and modern jurisprudence— all of which were to be collected, construed, debated, applied, and of course taught in the universities. Initially, the impulse to these researches was the demand for a richer basis for modern "interpretation," but concomitantly there arose a more purely "scientific" desire to reconstruct legal tradition as a fundamental part of national and indeed European culture. With such a mixture of motives A. M. Ducaurroy edited and translated Justinian's *Institutes* (1813 and many later editions) as an introduction to the Civil Code. A. J. Pardessus and

P. A. Fenet did the same with editions of the two greatest Enlightenment jurists, Chancellor D'Aguesseau (1819) and R. J. Pothier (1826) respectively, and Fenet again with an edition of the preliminary work for the code itself (1827).[27] The efforts of such scholarly lawyers, or lawyerly scholars, was an important aspect of the revival of historical studies in the early nineteenth century. Finally, Napoleon established in 1807 ten chairs of history, of which the most important was the "professor of the history of legislation," whose charge was to present "a tableau of various civil and criminal codes, political institutions, and public law adopted successively by other people down to the Napoleonic Code."[28]

Perhaps the most authoritative of the early commentaries was the treatise of Charles Toullier on "French civil law following the order of the Code," which well illustrates the conventional and conservative character of academic jurisprudence. Toullier begins, as Montesquieu had, with a discussion of "laws in general," with reference to other Old Regime authors, including Grotius, Pufendorf, Heineccius, and Blackstone (though not Vico), and to the provincial customs of Old Regime France. He also invoked natural law, but in a traditional legal sense rather than what he called the "metaphor" drawn from physical science, since jurisprudence was a human or "moral" science invested with values and aimed at justice.[29] For the most part his presentation was, like the Code itself in many respects, a rehash of modern Roman law (*usus modernus Pandectarum*, as German jurists liked to call it) as it had been taught for generations and was still being taught in France through the textbooks of Heineccius. In particular, Toullier preserved the Romanoid division of civil law into persons, things, and actions, though he did not hesitate to depart from and criticize Roman law in detail. He also tended to follow the Roman paternalistic conception of the family, likewise as a basis for a vaunted individual (adult male) "liberty" and even more conspicuously the Roman conception of "absolute property," though again natural law considerations, or at least rhetoric, came into play.[30] All of this was subor-

3. Charles Toullier. From A. J. Tonneau, *Un Jurisconsulte de transition: Charles Toullier (1752–1835) et son temps*. Photograph courtesy of Bibliothèque Nationale.

dinate, of course, to the political structure established by the Charter of 1815. With the accumulation of judicial experience and precedents and the emergence of new problems, Toullier's successors among the *grands commentateurs* found it necessary, in order to come to terms with modern society, to depart from this cautious "exegetical" model. Yet in many ways, they preserved the conservative tradition established by the pioneers of Napoleonic and Restoration jurisprudence.

Parallel and often converging with this upsurge of erudition was another tradition generated by the Code, namely, the *jurisprudence des arrêts* emanating from the Tribunal de Cassation established in 1790, which was another major source of "interpretation." The Tribunal, whose *Bulletin* began to appear in 1796, took part in the debates preliminary to the formation of the Code. Maintaining the position that interpretation was both "necessary" and a "true supplement to the laws," the Tribunal concerned itself especially with the disparity between "general utility" and the needs of particular localities. In 1804 the Tribunal became the Cour de Cassation; and its decisions, together with those of the Conseil d'Etat, constituted a running commentary on the Code and indeed, in the work of A. J. Coffinières, an "explication" of it.[31] As such, it would seem to be a danger to Napoleon's legislative designs, and in fact defenses of judicial power were not welcome in the imperial age. One celebration of "judicial power" written in 1807 could not be published until after the Emperor's abdication in May 1814, and even then under pretense of being "found" by a former redactor.[32] Nonetheless, the idea of judicial discretion was a cornerstone of the legal profession. It was defended most famously in a book by Henrion de Pansey, later president of the Cour de Cassation, and it promoted what some have regarded as the eventual "triumph" of that court in 1830, expressed in the principle of life tenure (*inamovibilité*) and in the implicit powers of "interpretation."[33]

The sense of history and of historical change embodied in this judicial tradition was nowhere expressed better than in the arguments of J.E.M. Portalis, one of those men, wrote

51

4. J.E.M. Portalis. From Lydie Schimséwitsch (Adolphe), *Portalis et son temps*. Photograph courtesy of University of North Carolina Library, Rare Book Collection, Chapel Hill.

Sainte-Beuve, "who have contributed to the restoration of society after convulsions and tempests." Portalis despised Rousseau's "false speculative philosophy" and the hubris of "Robespierrisme." On the contrary, he was a disciple of Montesquieu, a "political jurisconsult [Saint-Beuve continued] combining the magistrate with the legislator."[34] The face that Montesquieu presented to Portalis and most nineteenth-century scholars was that of the cautious, empirical- and historical-minded *parlementaire*, foe of a priori "system" and celebrator of Germanic tradition and immemorial "fundamental laws." In this view "natural law" was not universal reason but closer to the instinct defined by the Roman jurist Ulpian ("what nature teaches all animals") and expressed in diverse cultural forms according to historical and geographic factors. This interpretation, argued most persuasively by Montesquieu's editor, the Germanizing legal historian Edouard Laboulaye (whom we shall encounter later), was also the one preferred by Portalis.[35]

The Napoleonic Code gave new urgency to the polarity pointed out by Montesquieu, and Portalis tried to maintain the same conservative stance. There was a science of jurisprudence as well as legislation, Portalis believed, following the canons of Roman law, and it was the office of the former to determine the spirit (*le vrai sens*) of laws. Nor was it useful in the process of interpretation to destroy all tradition; rather, it was necessary "to honor the wisdom of our fathers, who formed the national character." Summing up his strategy, Portalis wrote, "The doctrine of the redactors was to conserve all that it was not necessary to destroy."[36] And thinking of Rousseau, he added, "New theories are only the systems of individuals; ancient maxims are the spirit of centuries past." Rome was not, nor could Napoleon's *imperium* be, built in a day, for "the codes of people are not made in a day; strictly speaking, they are not 'made' at all."[37] For such judgments Portalis was honored not only by members of the legal profession but also by later historians of law. According to one of the greatest of these, Henri Klimrath, Portalis had a "happy prescience" (*heureux pressentiment*) of the methods of the historical school of law, and there is no doubt that his conservative view of jurisprudence contributed at least indirectly to the "new history."[38]

Like the law schools, the law courts, especially the Cour de Cassation, gave a powerful impulse to the study of legal history in the nineteenth century. Among the scholars who served on this tribunal, Henrion de Pansey, Pardessus, Troplong, and Hello have already been encountered, and there will be others. One is Merlin de Douai, head of the Committee on Feudal Rights established in the wake of the "abolition" of feudalism on 4 August 1789, who later edited a serial collection of "questions of law" based not only on the decisions of the courts, but also on academic jurisprudence and historical sources going back to medieval times. There is no better illustration of the intersection between practical and academic jurisprudence, between law and history, than collections such as Merlin's intended as reference works for magistrates and advocates (except for, perhaps, the perennial standard, *Profession of Advocate* by Camus and Dupin). These collections constitute the very stuff of modern legal and, more selectively, social history, and are an example of how jurists sometimes help fix the patterns of historical interpretation by their selection of cases, decisions, principles, and even historical perspective.

If the Napoleonic Code gave impetus to a new wave of scholarship, it was even more central to one of the great ideological controversies of the nineteenth century: the debate over its own *raison d'être*. Was or was not a codified system of law like that of Justinian or Napoleon or the Prussian code of 1795 a proper mode for the organization of society? Could accumulated human experience be compressed into such an artificial container, or should a more flexible and perhaps equitable form of law be drawn from the past? This was the issue that for most of the century separated the philosophical school from the historical school of law—with jurists like Thibaut and Bentham on the one side, and Savigny and

Eichhorn on the other—and it was so seminal to history and the social sciences that one of the American founders of sociology saw fit to begin his pioneering study of the origins of his discipline with this debate.[39] The codification problem acted as a spur to historical thinking and investigating, and it served to define in the most precise and practical way the attitude of mind that came in the course of the nineteenth century to be defined as historicism. In no other context can we see more clearly the scholarly and conceptual collusion between Clio and Themis.

CHAPTER FIVE

The Legal Tradition

Optimum enim est legum interpres consuetudo.
—*Digest* 1.3.37

"History is the source of all human science," declared the jurist F. F. Poncelet in the public course he gave in 1820, "and the history of jurisprudence is the basis of the science of the legist."[1] This was in effect an axiom of legal studies in the Restoration, and the consequences were momentous for the legacy of the Enlightenment and of the Revolution. What this principle signified, not to put too fine a point on it, was simply a return to many of the assumptions, attitudes, methods, and materials of the Old Regime, even for lawyers who were busy summoning up a bourgeois future. "Our ancient constitution is the best commentary on the new," wrote the president of the Cour de Cassation in 1815, referring to the Charter of 1815 prefixed to the Civil Code.[2] As a summary of generations of legal theory and practice, the Code was a major conduit of prerevolutionary ideas and habits, but beyond this doctrinal embodiment of tradition there were at least three more dynamic vehicles of continuity with the Old Regime: the legal profession, reactionary (crypto- or neofeudal) ideology, and deep-seated traditions of legal and historical scholarship. Often inseparable, all of these agencies contributed to a sort of instinctive historical mentality that was a necessary precondition for the more self-conscious conceptualizing of the "new history."

Each aspect of this mentality is reflected in that "code of the profession of the advocate" first published in 1770 by Camus and for the last time over sixty years later by Dupin, a symbolic bridge doctrinally joining Enlightenment and July

Monarchy.[3] The professional chauvinism of the lawyer is displayed clearly in Camus' first letter "on the Order of Advocates . . . , as ancient as the legal system, as noble as virtue, as necessary as justice," and in a fragment added in 1818 by Dupin from D'Aguesseau "on the love of his estate." Also included by Dupin were various historical views of the profession, especially those of the feudist Antoine Loisel from the seventeenth century and of the encyclopedist Boucher d'Argis from the eighteenth. Obviously, the suppression of the legal profession in 1790 had not dampened its corporate ardor, nor would the chaotic period of *droit intermédiaire*. Old Regime hagiographies were continued in the nineteenth century after Napoleon's restoration of the profession by such works as J. F. Fournel's history of the advocates. With Fournel hagiography indeed became martyrology, as he prefaced one of his apologetic works with an honor roll of the profession in 1789 and a notice of several victims, including one *fusillé révolutionnairement* and another *décapité révolutionnairement*.[4] These he judged to be crimes of *lèse-nation*.

More typical, of course, were the survivors. Despite these unpleasant episodes, lawyers seemed on the whole to accommodate themselves remarkably well to political change and even professional extinction. If they could adapt themselves to Montesquieu (really quite an amateur), they could even accept Rousseau, for a while. Their lore and expertise set them apart even when the judiciary was opened to all citizens, and they continued to find positions in various tribunals and later in the schools of law established by Napoleon. The great Charles Toullier (after whom a street was named in 1854) was successively *philosophe*, revolutionary, Bonapartist, and monarchist, as well as pioneering commentator on the Civil Code—and he was not uncharacteristic of his profession.[5] In 1815 the law faculty shouted "Vive l'Empereur!" but welcomed his successor Louis XVIII in the "nineteenth year of his reign" even more enthusiastically with cries of "Vive le Roi! Vivent les Bourbons!"[6] In fact, lawyers seemed to be instinctive Talleyrands, displaying perhaps nostalgia for the past but for the

5. André Dupin. From André Dupin, *Eloge des douze magistrats,
1742–1829*. Photograph courtesy of Bibliothèque Nationale.

most part accommodating themselves to constitutional transformations. Their sense of history allowed them, in other
words, to move with the currents of change. It was not the
king or the republic that "never dies," to paraphrase the old
maxim; it was the legal profession.

One of the most flexible of all these "plastic careers" of
postrevolutionary lawyers was that of André Dupin ("*aîné*").
He came from a distinguished juridical family, his father a
member of the Legislative Assembly before having to flee from
the guillotine. Dupin himself, the first graduate of Napoleon's
law school, was a member of the restored *barreau* in 1802 and
of the restored Order of Advocates in 1810, becoming eventually both *bâtonnier*, in succession to Toullier in 1829, and
bibliothécaire of the Order, whence the bibliographical material
for his editions of Camus' handbook.[7] Under Napoleon he
had lamented the "terrible revolution" of 1789 that had destroyed so many institutions and schools, and in the Restoration he became known as the "lawyer of the marshals" because of his legitimist pleas. But in the revolution of 1830, as
counsel for an opposition newspaper, he leaned toward the
Orleanists. He was rewarded by an appointment as *procureur
général* of the Cour de Cassation and, in 1832, by admission
to the Academy. If he had any party allegiance, it was to the
Doctrinaires, but in fact his loyalties were extended most consistently to his beloved *Ordre* and to the grand tradition ex-
tending back some five centuries. To this tradition, too, were
dedicated most of his scholarly efforts, and he was largely
responsible for the revival of interest in Etienne Pasquier and
Antoine Loisel, among others. He was a living and teaching
embodiment both of the continuity of Old Regime and Restoration and of the intersection of law and history.

Inextricably bound up with professional chauvinism was
the endemic conservatism of lawyers. One critic may not have
been unfair in remarking, "Too bad for the feudists, the Par-
lementaires, and the Jesuits that M. Dupin was not a doctor
in 1798; the Revolution might never have taken place."[8] Underlying the antiquarian and hagiographic efforts of Fournel

was an extreme distaste for "the mania for reforms and innovations" and (with pejorative italics) "the speculations and *political theories*" of the Jacobins. J.E.D. Bernardi, a magistrate
and scholar exiled after Robespierre's fall, later complained of
"twenty-five years *without law*" and denounced anonymously
and belatedly the "Corsican domination" as even more destructive to institutions than the Revolution.[9] As for Toullier,
his biographer writes, "The mission of his life was to connect
the Civil Code to old French law."[10] As president of the Cour
de Cassation from 1810 to 1829, Henrion de Pansey carried
on the same campaign, and even more effectively. The handbook of Dupin sustained these conservative inclinations as well
as the sentimental traditions of the magistracy.

The ultimate power basis for the legal tradition was of course
judicial authority; and to a large extent the conservatism of
lawyers, as well as their understanding of the historical process, arose from their commitment to this social function. On
this practical level of judicial "interpretation" we can see one
of the principal social and intellectual links between the Old
Regime and the Restoration. By cleaving to the law, it was
possible to pass in good faith from feudist to republican to
Bonapartist to monarchist, and many jurists did so. Some,
indeed, never ceased being "feudists," though of course they
adapted their old mental habits to modern conditions. In consultations and commentaries on the Code, Toullier, the "modern Pothier" as Dupin called him, set about to restore neofeudal jurisprudence under the guise of "interpretation" and
especially the old civilian belief that "custom interprets law."[11]
He did this by means of the nice fiction established by his
colleague Merlin, or rather adapted by Merlin from Pothier
and older jurists, which distinguished between "dominant"
and "contractual feudalism" (*féodalité dominante, féodalité con-
tractante*). Among his consultations are defenses both of the
"seigneurial" right of *terrage* and the *dîme*, neither, he argued,
affected by the "abolition" of feudalism on the celebrated night
of 4 August 1789. The ghost of feudalism continued to haunt
the French countryside and law courts in the form of rents,

PIERRE PAUL HENRION DE PANSEY.

6. Henrion de Pansey. From Renée Laude, *Henrion de Pansey.*
Photograph courtesy of Columbia University Library.

servitudes, and other relics of the Old Regime. This spirit has
helped to animate modern historical scholarship as well.

This is illustrated even more strikingly by the career of
Henrion de Pansey, who started out as a wholly orthodox
member of the feudist tradition. Characteristically, he opposed the Maupeou Parlement and clung to the older conven-

tions of customary law, especially the program of the sixteenth-century jurist Charles Dumoulin, who had launched
the campaign to reform the abuses of feudalism (*complexum
feudale* was his term), but in the direction of national unity on
the basis of French custom rather than rationalization on the
basis of a Romanist legal science.[12] Apparently, Henrion was
too conservative even to be appointed to Merlin's committee
on feudalism, but he reemerged after the turn of the century
as a baron of the Empire and in 1810 as president of the Cour
de Cassation. Henrion had little interest in public law—legislative and executive, which he referred to as *droit politique*
and *droit des gens*—focusing instead on "civil law," by which
he meant that private sphere traditionally immune to interfer-
ence by governmental authority. In Hegelian terms, he was
concerned with civil society rather than the state, and his
commentaries frequently approach the level of social as well
as legal history. In a sense, he always remained a feudist.
Discussing the "seigneur" of a property, Henrion denied any
"intention of reviving the feudal idiom,"[13] but in fact, like
Toullier, he made his scholarship a haven of Old Regime jurisprudence.

   The defense of "judicial authority" was Henrion de Pansey's major task, especially after his appointment at the Cour
de Cassation and two years later (in 1812, at the age of sev-
enty!) as a member of the Emperor's council. To tyrannical
Romanist legislation Henrion opposed the Germanic inclination to judicial decisions, and in this connection he presented
a learned historical survey of the judiciary and cognate institutions from the Capetians down to the establishment of his
own tribunal, with particular emphasis on the "bourgeois liberties" created by the medieval communes. In conventional
terms, he celebrated his tradition as a cornerstone of "tem-
pered monarchy" and those "fundamental laws" that for centuries had guarded against popular as well as royal absolut-
ism. Citing jurists from Bodin (and Machiavelli) to
Montesquieu, he insisted that "the prince should never med-
dle with the affairs of the judiciary."[14] This was why life-

tenure for judges (*inamovibilité*) was so essential. In Henrion's mind, then, and especially in his scholarship, the judiciary was a primary vehicle not only of legal continuity with the Old Regime but also of a proper understanding of the historical process.

Even the institutional innovations of the Revolution Henrion was able to defend in traditionalist terms, most notably in his pioneering work on the justices of the peace (*juges de paix*). "The legislators who gave us the justices of the peace," he wrote, "are worthy of the greatest praise. They wanted to reestablish for us that primitive magistracy [*cette magistrature des premières âges*] . . . , which was guided by example and judged by the authority of reason alone."[15] This office was the "altar of unity" (*autel de la concorde*) for each *arrondissement*, concerned with local civil suits, especially disputes over possession of land and problems of trespass. Although established in 1792, this institution drew upon ancient customs regarding "possessory actions" going back to the work of Philippe de Beaumanoir and the *Establishments of Saint Louis* in the thirteenth century. In general, Henrion celebrated this jurisdiction, analogous to that long respected in England, as something restored from the age of society before the afflictions of codification and as a reflection of the enduring variety and complexity of French tradition. Henrion's perspective, though originating in attitudes closer to those of Montesquieu and Boulainvilliers, seemed in agreement with those of Romanticism. In 1826 one contributor to the *Globe* judged Henrion de Pansey to be "a worthy member, along with Savigny, of the historical school."[16]

Another surviving jurist from the Old Regime, a somewhat more enlightened survivor, was Bernardi, whose attack on "Buonaparte" has already been mentioned. Perhaps a main reason for his intellectual longevity (from the 1770s to the Restoration) was his affection for what he persisted in calling the "revolutions" of European history.[17] Of such revolutions, however, he took an extraordinarily legalistic view, after the fashion of Montesquieu's chapters on the "origin and revolutions" of Roman succession law and French civil law. In 1775 he associated the term with his hopes for the reform of the legal system, and even in 1807, while speaking of "the great revolutions of the sixteenth century," he was thinking as much of legal scholarship as of religion and politics. From his early prize essay on Jacques Cujas, "the restorer of jurisprudence," to his laudatory study of Michel de L'Hôpital, contemporary of Cujas and reformer of French law, Bernardi placed his hopes in jurisprudence, which was "in effect the accumulated wisdom from all the ages," for "cette heureuse révolution."[18]

In 1803, even before promulgation of the Code, Bernardi produced a pioneering work on modern French law based on a course given at Napoleon's Academy of Legislation. Here he expressed the opinion, or hope, that the new effort of codification was the offspring not of the "revolutionary spirit" of Cambacérès but of a long line of French and Roman attempts at codification, especially those of Jean Domat and Chancelier D'Aguesseau. It was to be continually modified by judicial wisdom (l'équité du juge) of the same corporation of experts whose quasi-priestly function (a reference to the Roman formula sacerdotes legum; prêtres de la justice) was to preserve and extend the legacy of legal and historical learning. Bernardi was disgusted at the way in which the "barbarous system" of the Napoleonic Code and its sycophantic commentators, such as Locré, violated the "ancient constitution" of France; and he expressed his opposition with reference to the sixteenth-century work of Claude de Seyssel as well as to modern authors such as Edmund Burke.

A final example of the intellectual continuity encouraged by professional lawyers is that of P.L.C. Gin, a monarchist who had the temerity after escaping from prison to publish a defense of Louis XVI two years after the king's execution. In characteristic style, Gin presented a "reasoned analysis" of French law in the hope of giving organization to the mélange of Romano-Germanic customs.[19] Neither revolution nor Bonapartism could change his goals. The first edition of his book was a comparative study of Roman and customary law according to the "natural order" of Domat, while the 1804 edition, while following and amplifying "the new code of the French," was not changed in any significant way. He relied in particular on the interpretations of Portalis and argued that the Code proved both the dominance of Romanism in French society and the impossibility of legislation by the "million-headed hydra" of revolution. For Gin and many other like-minded jurists, even the Civil Code, advertised by Bonapartists as a fulfillment of the Revolution, was a confirmation and continuation of the deepest French traditions.

In general, the French legal tradition, both the practical and the academic branches, had a deep commitment to historical scholarship; and some aspects of the nineteenth-century revival were simply taking up Old Regime concerns forgotten in the heat of revolutionary activity. In retrospect, the golden age seemed to have been above all the sixteenth century, when the two giants of French jurisprudence were establishing their reputations and indeed what three centuries later would become scholarly legends. The first was Jacques Cujas, dominating figure of the "French method," as legal humanism was called; and the other was Charles Dumoulin, who "was to French law," as Camus wrote, "what Cujas was to Roman law."[20] Cujas' career was documented and celebrated in a groundbreaking biography by Jacques Berriat-Saint-Prix, a book that was translated into German by Ernst Spangenberg and that led Savigny to break off his own planned work. Cujas' symbolic and indeed eponymous position as founder of "Jurisprudence Cujaciana" (in Dupin's words) was fixed with the naming of the old rue Saint-Etienne-des-Grès after him in 1865 and later the library of the Ecole de Droit on that street.[21] Dumoulin preserved not only his antifeudal and antiecclesiastical "legend" but also, through jurists like Henrion de Pansey, his authority in the nineteenth century.[22] Other sixteenth-century scholars who benefited from this juridico-antiquarian revival of interest were Etienne Pasquier, lauded by Sainte-Beuve as archetype of the legist tradition (as well as champion of French poetry), and his friend and colleague Antoine Loisel, whose historical celebration of the tradition, appropriately entitled *Pasquier*, was republished in Dupin's *Profession of Advocate*. Both Pasquier and Loisel were subjects of the annual *éloges* delivered before the Cour de Cassation. The professional continuity of the legal profession over the centuries is vividly illustrated in the portraits of L'Hôpital, D'Aguesseau, Henrion de Pansey, Dumoulin, Cujas, and others decorating the gallery of the Cour de Cassation, for which Dupin gave an oration in 1836.[23]

Restoration France also saw a revival of interest in the legal monuments of the Middle Ages, including the *Establishments of Saint Louis*, the records of the Parlement (starting with the so-called *Olim*), the works of Beaumanoir and other feudists, and especially the ordinances of the monarchy of the Old Regime. In this great "document-hunt" François Isambert and his colleagues in 1821 started publishing a monumental collection of legislation from Carolingian times down to 1789, while Pardessus later completed the still more ambitious series begun in the seventeenth century.[24] Other examples of Old Regime series taken up again after a revolutionary hiatus include the *Gallia Christiana* and the *Histoire littéraire de la France*, in which Daunou was heavily involved. Enlightenment scholars continued also to be valued and published, among them Domat, D'Aguesseau, Pothier, of course Montesquieu, and the German jurist J. G. Heineccius, whose textbooks were translated into French and used in law courses well into the nineteenth century.[25] Antiquarian studies were promoted not only in the university and the law faculty but also in scholarly organizations such as the Société des Antiquaires de France (formed in 1813), the Académie des Inscriptions et Belles-lettres (restored in 1816), the Ecole des Chartes (founded in 1822), and the Société de l'Histoire de France (established by Guizot a decade later).[26] All of these "great historical enterprises" in their own way established scholarly bridges between the Old Regime and modern France. Nor had the style changed that much, for as Heine remarked about the *éloge* given by Mignet for Daunou in 1843, one would have judged it appropriate to the age of Louis XIV except for the absence of powdered wigs.[27]

The most concrete link with the Old Regime was probably the archival tradition, which by Napoleon's time was professionally over five centuries old. From the start, the archives represented a major target of the Revolution, whether as a symbol and repository of "servitudes" to be destroyed or as a cache of titles to be taken over from the dismantled corporations and distributed by revolutionary legislation. Appointed as first archivist by the Convention in 1790, A. G. Camus fought to preserve his charge from being demolished or despoiled until his death, and succeeded at least in forming the basis for the "historical section."[28] In 1804 he was succeeded by Daunou, who added manuscripts from the collections of subject states (including Spain and the Vatican), separated the national archives from the Corps Législatif and found a home for them in 1808 in the Hôtel Soubise, and continued the work of centralization and classification (though the judicial archives were not transferred from the Sainte-Chapelle until 1817). Napoleon took a personal interest in collecting the relics not only of his own but of more ancient national "glory," and he planned an archival "palace" to exhibit them.

Camus' directorship was interrupted during the Restoration. Under the regime of his successor La Rue, himself an émigré, records were restored to other émigrés such as the future Charles X, and to the despoiled foreign collections, and some were even lost through unauthorized sale of parchments. Daunou himself taught history during the Restoration, and his conception of archival tradition figures prominently in the course he gave at the Collège de France in 1819 on "historical criticism" and the sources of historical studies, and in his later lectures on historical method (*art d'écrire l'histoire*) and historiography.[29] After the revolution of 1830, Daunou returned as director of the archives and two years later was joined by Michelet, who extended efforts into the departmental collections and made the archives a major source of his "resurrection" of the French past.[30]

The French legal tradition, strengthened by the Restoration, involved both scholarly continuity and ideological carry-overs, perhaps most notably old debates about the ultimate provenance of French institutions and culture. The issue generally turned on the relative significance of the Roman and the French (which is to say Germanic) legacies, the extremes neatly represented by Cujas and Dumoulin respectively; and of course it had implications for legal ideals as well as historical interpretation. The Roman model was advocated by humanists like Cujas and natural law philosophers like Domat, as well as by other contributors to the revolutionary and Bonapartist legislation. In the eighteenth century Romanism was defended enthusiastically by the Abbé Dubos and, among others, the jurists Claude Henrys and J. Bouhier, president of the Parlement of Dijon.[31] These men were all monarchists, and yet it is hardly going too far to say that their legal assumptions—especially that Roman law was reason incarnate (*ratio scripta; raison écrite*)—won the day in the preliminary discussions to the Civil Code. In historical scholarship Romanism was less successful but still continued to attract adherents, including Dubos' remote successor Fustel de Coulanges.

On the other side were the "Germanists," who included an even more distinguished line of scholars, such as Boulainvilliers, Mably, Boucher d'Argis, and above all Montesquieu. Inclining toward this position, too, were many of the professors of French law, installed by an edict of 1679 and charged with defining French law strictly in terms of the *coutumes* and royal *ordonnances*.[32] In the southern provinces ("of written law") especially, they were the ideological as well as academic rivals of the better established professors of civil law, who could hardly avoid a Romanist bias. The professors of French law made their own contributions to legal unification, most notably in their effort to extract the "spirit" of national law from indigenous traditions, including the *jurisprudence des arrêts* as well as the work of feudists like Dumoulin and Loisel. Several of the redactors were numbered among their students, including Portalis and Merlin, and in various ways the nineteenth-century historians of French law may be regarded as their doctrinal descendants.

The Germanists were supported in their efforts by feudists from the northern provinces ("of customary law"). One of the most effective champions of native traditions was an *érudit* of Troyes, Pierre Groseley, *paysan* and biographer of Pierre Pithou, probably the greatest jurist-historian of the sixteenth century. Writing in the mid-eighteenth century, Groseley took pains to declare that his perspective was quite independent of Montesquieu and derived instead from traditional researches into legal tradition along lines set by generations of feudists beginning with Dumoulin. Groseley defended his conservatism not only against rationalists but also against Romanists like Bouhier, who had not learned that "the particular *esprit* of our customary law is to be found in the manners and usages of the ancient inhabitants of northern Gaul," though to be sure they had changed over the centuries.[33] These attitudes, displayed especially in the discussion of controversies over the origin of feudalism, of the nobility and its privileges, of the legal profession, and even of the bourgeoisie, carried over into the scholarship of the nineteenth century and indeed tended to reinforce the more sophisticated medievalism of that period. Several of the Enlightenment Germanizers, most notably Mlle de Lézardière and C. J. Perreciot, were republished then and contributed further to the intellectual continuity demanded by the legal tradition.[34] Perhaps the most striking illustration of this was the debate between Romanists and Germanists, which not only persisted but reached a high point in the Romantic age.

Such were some of the native sources of historical jurisprudence and of legal history that reemerged in the first quarter of the nineteenth century. Yet the conceptual results were not impressive to many observers. There were widespread complaints about the state of French legal and historical scholarship in the wake of Revolution, Bonapartism, and the demise of the ancient faculties of law. The charges of Chateaubriand, and even more of Mme de Staël about the distressing condition of historical studies were, though ideologically inspired, not unjust. As for jurisprudence, Dacier's report of 1808 noted the "infinity" of commentaries already accumulated, but like Napoleon he thought them mostly bookish fictions (*spéculations du librairie*) and detrimental if not useless to practical jurisprudence.[35] In the Restoration students still began their studies with antiquated textbooks like that of Heineccius, or perfunctory summaries of Roman law like that of Dupin; and the persistence of natural-law attitudes, for instance in the guise of Benthamism or Destutt de Tracy's "ideology," was hardly conducive to a historical spirit. Nor did French jurists even have a comprehensive theory of legal interpretation to apply to their six codes and the endless juridical and social repercussions.

In 1819 A. J. L'Herbette offered some explanations for "the stagnation of the science of law in France."[36] One was the divorce of law from other disciplines, another the argumentative method encouraged by the commentators and, last but not least, the lack of official, which is to say financial, support. In fact, the teaching of law was very limited. The first chair of legal history, established in 1819, was dropped in 1822 (as was a chair of political economy), and neither the proposal for reinstatement in 1827 nor that in 1838 was followed up for another generation.[37] L'Herbette also recognized the discouraging effects of political instability; but unfortunately his remedy, an antiquated form of Baconian empiricism, hardly seemed adequate responses to the crisis he detected. Eight years later, despite advances in the teaching especially of Roman law, J.L.E. Ortolan could still complain that legal scholarship in France had "remained stationary" in both the *barreau* and the faculties of law.[38]

Clearly the old legal tradition—just like the old historiography, and at precisely the same time—needed resuscitation. Indeed the forces that were acting to bring this about in both fields were already operating in the 1820s. As a "new history" was being proclaimed by Thierry and others, a new jurisprudence was also being fashioned, and likewise fashioned in many ways in the progressive image of the *bourgeois conqué-rants*. Guizot's friend, law professor Raymond Troplong, who contributed to the alliance between Clio and Themis by a manifesto "on the necessity of restoring historical studies to French law," made the ideological connection, too. In modern times jurisprudence was not limited to citing Pothier or even the Code, he wrote in 1835, for this would be to "violate the law of progress and forget that a science that advances is a science that expands."[39] In the Restoration period this expansion came about in large part through an intellectual impulse originating in Germany.

The German Impulse

*

> Der Staat ist ein Organismus, der nicht
> gemeistert und fabriciert werden kann, sondern
> sich entwickelt und gleidert.
>
> —Schelling

The crisis of jurisprudence, which was still regarded widely
as the major science of society, went deeper than pedagogy,
methodology, and even financing. It was an ideological problem with international as well as national dimensions. Put
crudely and in terms of public opinion, France seemed to have
violated the deepest traditions of European society: 1789 betrayed social order, 1792 betrayed political conventions, 1794
betrayed human values, and 1804, to listen to some of Napoleon's critics, betrayed everything, especially the future of the
family of European nations. Conservatives, liberals, and "socialists" alike agreed that the times of the Caesars, of Justinian, were past, and that the task of jurisprudence was to fulfill
the social ideals of the new age (whatever they were). Not
that Napoleon, or the old revolutionaries for that matter, dis-
agreed with this; but his, and their, authoritarian style of-
fended intellectuals and professionals of many persuasions. The
criticisms of Chateaubriand and Mme de Staël set the tone for
the outburst of vilification that the Restoration produced—
and that contributed to the Napoleonic legend, the antithesis
of the ideal of the "social."

Of all those who had been victimized by Napoleon's legislative designs, administrative impositions, and of course military intrusions, the Germans were the most reflective and
articulate in their antagonism. Law, to the Germans, was ultimately the product not of sovereign will but of custom. "In
Germany all culture comes from the people," Fichte declared

in 1807, and went on to deplore the "evil associations and seductive.power of vanity" that "have swept the growing nation into spheres which are not its own."[1] The Germans had resisted the ancient Romans; they must do the same against the modern Romanizers with their false rationalism. Hardly better than the invading armies were the administrative reforms introduced by Napoleon and especially the Code. Although some jurists respected and taught French law in German universities, others rejected it, among them the Hanoverian August counsellor Rehberg, embittered by the incorporation of his state into the Kingdom of Westphalia. In 1814 Rehberg published a denunciation of the Napoleonic Code that won the praise of Savigny in his much more famous pamphlet of that same year on the problem of codification.[2] In general, it is not surprising that the impulse to reconstruct jurisprudence—to restore in particular the connections between legal philosophy and history, between law and life—came from this quarter. The German impulse took many forms, but what is significant here is that many-sided intellectual movement that came to be known as the historical school of law.[3]

The intellectual revolution, in a sense counterrevolution, in Germany had been brewing long before Mme de Staël's *De l'Allemagne* of 1810, and in fact France had not been wholly immune from "the German mirage" even before this.[4] Two of the earliest missionaries were Joseph Degérando and Charles de Villers, who in 1808 (like Dacier) submitted a bibliographical report, this one on the state of literature and history in Germany, and who wrote a study of Luther as a founder of Germanic "liberty."[5] An even more influential promoter of Germanism was their younger friend Guizot. Among jurists, Citizen (Count) Portalis came into contact with German scholarship during his Swiss exile of 1798 to 1800. In a posthumously published book on "the use and abuse of the philosophic spirit," he presented an extensive critique of Kant and an appreciation of Herder, Pütter, Schmidt, and other *Vorläufer* of the historical school, whose views no doubt reinforced his own moderate approach to the formation of the French

Code.[6] Interest in German ideas of history was even more apparent in the work of Portalis's son. He accompanied Portalis into exile and in 1800 published an essay on *The Duty of a Historian*, arguing that instead of interpreting the past literally or philosophically, scholars should "consider the genius and character of each century in judging great men and separate them from the errors and prejudices of their time."[7] This was one of the first lessons of the historical school.

Even under Napoleon, then, some French intellectuals were reading German books. In 1804 Gustav Hugo, founder of the historical school, was admitted to the Academy of Legislation (of which Portalis was president).[8] The work of Eichhorn was known to both Villers and Dacier; and of course German works on jurisprudence, not only those of Heineccius but also commentaries on the Napoleonic Code such as those of K. S. Zachariae, J.A.L. Seidensticker, and (in Latin) Ernst Spangenberg must have been known to jurists. But the full impact of Germanism and other byproducts of émigré culture did not come until the Restoration and the reestablishment, with some qualifications, of the old "Republic of Letters" on which the Enlightenment had presumably been built. A major agency of Germanist influence came by way of the university, especially through the missionary lectures of critics of the Restoration monarchy such as Guizot and his colleague Victor Cousin, who popularized the work of Kant, Hegel, and even Creuzer (whose translated work on ancient religion was dedicated to Cousin).[9] Cousin's Sorbonne lectures, especially from 1818 and again from 1828, contributed not only to historical thought but also, at least indirectly, to legal scholarship through the encouragement he gave to his young colleagues Quinet and Michelet, translators and to some extent disciples, respectively, of Herder and Vico.[10] In that same year the Belgian jurist J. D. Meyer published his cosmopolitan study of European judicial institutions, displaying an unusual familiarity with German scholarship and the contemporary debate over codification.[11] He did not recognize a particular "school" but did grasp the drift of opinion reflected in the works of Justus

Möser, Eichhorn, Savigny, and others; and in this connection he cited the old adage of Montesquieu that "it is necessary to illuminate laws by history, and history by laws." Hardly less important for this goal were the groundbreaking studies of Roman history by the greatest of all representatives of historical criticism of the age, Barthold Georg Niebuhr, whose study of Roman history (translated finally into French in 1830) was long before Ranke a model for the new history of the nineteenth century.

But these were all minor winds of doctrine, eddies of scholarship, compared to the intellectual storms accompanying the central invasion of Germanism in the Restoration. For jurisprudence, one of the glaring omissions in Mme de Staël's manifesto, the aftermath of Napoleon witnessed two spectacular events in the world of learning. One was the emergence of Niebuhr's and Eichhorn's younger colleague Friedrich Karl von Savigny as the leading figure in German, and indeed European, legal thought and scholarship. This was signaled by the publication of his manifesto "On the Vocation of Our Age for Legislation and Jurisprudence" (1814), which represented a major critique of current ideas of codification, and by the appearance the next year of his (and Eichhorn's) journal for a historical science of law, the *Zeitschrift für geschichtliche Rechtswissenschaft*, which became the leading organ of legal scholarship and criticism.[12] The second event, the year following, was Niebuhr's discovery of a manuscript of Gaius' *Institutes* (2d century A.D.), the only full text of any pre-Justinian work. This miraculous disinterment symbolized as well as signalized the reconstruction of European jurisprudence in much the same way as Petrarch's discovery of Cicero's *Familiares* did the revival of classical antiquity. More than that, the Gaian text, restored from a medieval palimpsest and published for the first time in 1820, gave a direct impulse to the scholarly labors carried on by the avant-garde of legal science headed by Savigny.

The deeper context of the historical school of law in Germany was the rise of "historicism" (a word coined in the early

75

nineteenth century, not in the later part, as Meinecke had thought).[13] Historicism *avant la lettre* had been reflected not only in J. G. Herder's famous philosophizing about history but also in the scholarly productions of German universities, especially that of Göttingen. Historians such as Möser, J. C. Gatterer, and Ludwig Schlözer were turning from politics and war to the study of institutions and society long before the "new history" of Restoration France.[14] Aside from theology and perhaps classical scholarship, jurisprudence was probably the field most affected by historicism. Jurists like J. S. Pütter and Ludwig Spittler, preferring the "good old law" of the German Reich to natural law confections and the concrete investigations of Montesquieu to the rationalist superficialities of Voltaire, reinforced the sophistication and of course the conservatism of the historians.

The man usually recognized as founder of the historical school of law was Pütter's student Gustav Hugo, professor at Göttingen from 1788, whose implicitly counterrevolutionary treatise began to appear, appropriately enough, in 1789.[15] Hugo's book was soon reinforced by his own journal, the immensely successful *Civilistisches Magazin*, which reviewed most juridical works of significance during the first third of the nineteenth century. He also gained renown (as Guizot later did) by association with Edward Gibbon, through his translation into German of the famous forty-fourth chapter on Roman law. He followed this with his own history of Roman law, the first modern critical study.[16] Hugo's major goal was above all a "philosophy of positive law"; and his "juristic encyclopedia" was based on an evolutionary "juristic anthropology" that he regarded as standing in the same relation to law as metaphysics did to general philosophy. For Hugo philosophy and positive law had long been at odds, since they had the same relationship as ideals had with reality; and it was his aim, through history, to bring them finally into harmony. Without a historical base, Hugo argued, law was "mere metaphysics" (*bloss Metaphysik*).[17] Like Herder, he opposed the imposition of the methods of natural science upon the social—

or in terms more appropriate to that age, "moral"—sciences. This was the conceptual justification for historicism, especially in the field of jurisprudence.

But it was Hugo's younger friend Friedrich Karl von Savigny who took over leadership of the *Historische Rechtsschule*. In 1803, at the age of twenty-four, he published an extraordinary monograph on the Roman law of possession, displaying at once his mastery over the sources of legal history and his concern for the adaption of civil law to modern conditions.[18] The next year he paid a visit to Paris with his disciple Jakob Grimm and was cordially received by Dacier, then curator of manuscripts. In 1810 he joined the faculty of the newly founded University of Berlin and from the chair of jurisprudence carried on his championship of the cause of historicism in the law. The great debate, the *Kodifikationsstreit*, was set off by the pamphlet written by Rehberg against the Napoleonic legislation. It became an international *cause célèbre* with Thibaut, professor of law at the University of Heidelberg, who defended a philosophical (that is, natural-law) approach to legal interpretation and who advocated a German code on this basis. In 1814 Savigny responded with his famous manifesto, "The Vocation of Our Age for Legislation and Jurisprudence," denying that the time was ripe for such a philosophical enterprise.[19]

Others entered the debate, among the most vociferous Jeremy Bentham, whose "Codification Proposal" circulated in 1822 "to all nations professing Liberal Opinions."[20] No one could withstand his utilitarian logic, Bentham asserted, except "corruptionists" and "knaves," which is to say lawyers. Some followers of the "philosophical school," feeling threatened by the irrationalist implications of historicism, joined in as well. Hegel argued, "No greater insult could be offered to a civilized people or to its lawyers than to deny them ability to codify their law; for such ability cannot be that of constructing a legal system with a novel content, but only that of apprehending . . . the content of existing laws. . . ."[21] In Germany the controversy did not cease until the adoption of the *Bürgerliches Gesetzbuch* in 1900.

The position of the historical school was stated most authoritatively by Savigny, and it began with a critique of the Napoleonic Code, which "broke into Germany, and ate in, further and further, like a cancer. . . ."[22] Yet although the Code was a political instrument designed "as a bond to fetter nations," Savigny's own criticisms of it were mostly legal and social and based above all on the "preparatory work" to the codification. While it was modeled on Roman law, French jurisprudence was primitive by comparison, and so was the attendant scholarship. "I myself," recalled Savigny, "have heard a law professor in Paris say that the books of Cujas, it was true, could not be omitted in a complete library, but that they were no longer necessary because all that was good in them is to be found in Pothier." Even more ridiculous was the belief of another jurist that two great sixteenth-century scholars, Lipsius and Sicardus, were contemporaries respectively of the Twelve Tables and the Theodosian Code. All too often the appeal of French jurists to "equity" or "natural law" was a cover for ignorance and unprofessionalism.

On such soil what fruit could grow? There was precious little legal "science," despite all the talk of natural law, and less understanding of history, so essential to a regular jurisprudence. Since former law had been abrogated, judges were free to follow old usages, whether civilian or customary, and the result was that prerevolutionary diversity and irregularity were in various ways increased. Savigny did not hesitate to point out the lack of legal expertise of almost all of the redactors, including Portalis and Maleville as well as Cambacérès.[23] What they had done was simply to plunder civil law and the works of Pothier. No wonder their law, especially the new property law based on a distortion of the Roman conception, was in a state of chaos. Savigny could only repeat the conclusion made by one of the conservative magistrates from the court of appeal of Montpellier, who had warned against "an incomplete system of legislation . . . joined to a defective jurisprudence." But of course Savigny set his arguments in the framework of a broader conception of legal history. For without history, he taught, system was impossible.

In Germany things were different. "A historical spirit has been everywhere awakened," Savigny wrote of the offspring of historicism, "and leaves no room for the shallow self-sufficiency above alluded to." He insisted on the twofold nature of law: "first, as part of the aggregate existence of the community, which it does not cease to be, and second, as a distinct branch of knowledge in the hands of the jurists."[24] In general, "law grows with the growth and strengthens with the strength of nations," he declared, "and finally dies away as the nation loses its nationality." In Germany law continued to express the "common life of the nation"—Herder's *Volksgeist*, which itself had associations with civilian concepts of custom (*consuetudo*)—but had not yet reached the status of a true science; and so the codification movement was premature, though perhaps less so than in France. It was the task and destiny of the *Historische Rechtsschule*, Savigny believed, to remedy this historical deficiency.

The year after this manifesto (which was also the year of Waterloo), Savigny's dominant position in the historical school was signaled both by his new journal and by the appearance of the first volume of his monumental history of Roman law in the Middle Ages.[25] In part a contribution to German "historical science," this work was also an attempt to reconstruct legal tradition for the practical purposes of modern jurisprudence (*usus modernus pandectarum*). Savigny took an active interest in the movement for legal reform and in 1840 became Minister of Justice for the reform of the Prussian *Landrecht*. In his later years he published six volumes of another monumental work, a "system of modern Roman law," which represented a sort of theoretical counterpart to the history, though still based on historicist principles. Indeed this work was, or would have been if completed, Savigny's answer to the challenge he issued in 1814, his formulation of the mature, Romanist jurisprudence prerequisite to any successful code.

Throughout his life Savigny carried on the attack, or counterattack, against the "philosophical," alias "unhistorical," school, represented first by Thibaut and later by Gans (under the spiritual protection of Hegel). The young Karl Marx was a witness and to some degree a product of the *Methodenstreit* waged by his two teachers and their followings, Savigny with the "realists" and Gans with the "idealists," first in the classroom and then in the late 1830s in published form.[26] Repercussions of the debate were also felt in France, and the jurisprudence of the Code is filled with the issues and interpretations of the historical and philosophical schools.

The central purpose of Savigny's and Hugo's doctrine was to provide a modern, expert, and empirical alternative to the rationalist legacy of Jacobinism and Bonapartism. In more positive terms, however, it also suggested a philosophy of history and of law-making. "What is the influence of the past on the present?" is the way Savigny phrased the question, and "What is the relation of what is now to what will be?"[27] In a sense, Savigny was offering a philosophical justification for the process of judicial (and academic) "interpretation" in its continuing rivalry with the process of legislative (and executive) "action." That law needed practical "interpretation" rather than rationalistic explanation was best shown by comparison with language—which was always, for Savigny, the closest analogy. Law and language had practically identical historical trajectories, from preliterate (oral tradition and custom) to articulate (prose discourse and written laws) to rational (philosophy and systematic jurisprudence). Both arose from usage and popular belief (*Volksglaube*), "therefore, through the imperceptible impact of inherent forces, not through the arbitrary decision of a legislator."

So it was that hermeneutics was central to the historical school. The philosophical and theological theory of interpretation was enjoying a new flowering precisely in this age of German historicism and nascent Romanticism, most notably in the work of Savigny's colleagues at the University of Berlin, Wolf and Schleiermacher. This was no less true, though much less appreciated, of legal hermeneutics, also a product ultimately of sixteenth-century scholarship. One example was K. S. Zachariae, professor of law at the University of Heidelberg, whose *Hermeneutik* appeared in 1805.[28] At that time, Zachariae was lecturing on the Napoleonic Code; and through his textbook and that of Ernst Spangenberg, German theories of interpretation, especially those of the philosophical school, were introduced to French scholars. Hermeneutical discussions were intensified by the translation into French in 1811 of Thibaut's *Theory of Logical Interpretation* and subsequent criticisms and assaults from members of the historical school, culminating in that of Savigny himself in his "system" of 1840.[29]

Legal hermeneutics was implicitly significant for the massive enterprise of reconstructing legal history but explicitly necessary for the status of "legal science." To natural law conceptions, whether revolutionary or imperial, Savigny opposed a historical view resting on older traditions and in effect demanding a critical understanding of law analogous to the "higher criticism" of the Bible preached, and to some extent practiced, by Schleiermacher. Like the Bible, the law (especially Roman law) contained lacunae, interpolations, and obscurities that cried out for historical reconstruction. Also like the Bible, Roman (and Romanoid) law was associated with an authoritarian tradition that obstructed such historical "interpretation," and Savigny devoted himself to breaking down such obstruction. This was only preliminary, however, to the major purpose of legal science, which had always been to establish the "spirit of law" (*mens legum* in the old civilian phrase; *esprit des lois* in Domat's and Montesquieu's more familiar rendering) and to join social reality to legal ideals. In this endless task, the true expert was the jurist, the legal "scientist."[30] Historical scholarship was at least an indirect beneficiary of this central lesson of the historical school of law.

This was the Romanist aspect of the German impulse, and because of its international implications (Roman law had been the "common law" of all European nations except England), it has deserved priority. But hardly less important in the postrevolutionary age was the national aspect, especially since medieval customs had always been opposed to the foreign intrusions of Roman traditions. The leading figures in the effort to revive Germanic legal tradition were two of Savigny's closest colleagues, J. G. Eichhorn and Jakob Grimm. A student of Hugo as well, Eichhorn began to publish his pioneering history of German law in 1808, an impressive parallel to Savigny's survey of Roman law in the Middle Ages.[31] The legal implications of Eichhorn's work in history and private law were even more disturbing to many advocates of codification, since the suggestion was that national and local customs were the true reflection of the "spirit of the laws," or rather, the spirit of the people (*Volksgeist*). In several ways, Eichhorn represents both the culmination of Göttingen historiography and a partner, with Hugo and Savigny, in the historical school of law.

Grimm, one of Savigny's first students at Marburg, accompanied him in 1805 to Paris on a scholarly visit and in the course of investigations into German folk literature and language became interested in legal antiquities as an expression of national spirit. Along with Savigny he was convinced of the cultural congruence of language and law, and in 1815 he published an essay on "poetry in law" before turning his efforts to the sources of medieval German law.[32] Grimm's *Antiquities of German Law* was "a very difficult book," according to Michelet, "in which all the dialects, all the ages of this language have revealed the symbols, the formulas by which the various Germanies have consecrated the great actions of human life (birth, marriage and death, wills, sales, homage, etc.)."[33] For Grimm law, no less than literature and language, was an "expression of society"; the judge (*Richter*) no less than the poet (*Dichter*) was a spokesman for the popular mind. Following the mythological studies of Creuzer as well as the interpretations of Herder, Grimm proposed through his "symbolic method" to deduce from legal sources basic patterns of society and culture. In this enterprise the focus of the historical school tended to shift from legal practice to historical scholarship, and in fact professional jurists tended to view such efforts with suspicion. This, as we shall see, is where Michelet came in.

"The French do well to study and to translate our writers," wrote Goethe in 1824, "for limited as they are both in form and motives, they can only look without for means."[34] This had been the message of Mme de Staël, and during the 1820s it was being received in many quarters. The "German voyage" was becoming almost as important for young French intellectuals as the "Italian voyage" was for Germans. Quinet and Michelet paid their first visits in 1827 and 1828 respectively. They were also lifelong friends, driven originally to "Teutomania" (as Quinet later jokingly referred to it) through the encouragement of Cousin and his Eclecticism.[35] Another prominent young Germanizer was Saint-Marc Girardin, who succeeded Guizot at the Sorbonne and gave a popular course on "The Political and Literary History of Germany." He visited Gans in Berlin in 1830 (a year before Hegel's death), talked with him in the Tiergarten, and later wrote an appreciation of this "particular friend of France."[36] "I dream of a political alliance."[37] He pointed out the particular importance of Germanism for the new history, which he contrasted sharply with the "false colors" of the traditional "court historian."

For jurisprudence and legal history the "German impulse" was absolutely essential and came into prominence with the generation of 1830. In this connection, Chateaubriand pointed out the rivalry between the "philosophical-historical party" led by Hegel and the purely "historical party" of Niebuhr and Savigny, "who traced the history of Roman law from its poetic age down to the philosophical age at which we have now arrived."[38] An even more effective popularizer of these schools was Eugène Lerminier, who came from Strasbourg and had already studied in Germany before enrolling in the Ecole de Droit in Paris. In 1827 Lerminier published his thesis on Savigny, entered into correspondence with Hegel and Gans, and began preparations for an immensely popular course on the history of legal philosophy, which he began giving in 1829.[39]

The German impulse was transmitted also by visits paid in the 1820s by Hegel and Gans, by immigrants like Heinrich Heine, and above all by scholarship of such Germanists as Henri Klimrath (another Strasbourgeois) and Edouard Laboulaye.[40] It was in the climate created by such cultural interpenetration that both historical and legal scholarship in France began to expand their concerns. This was another condition not only of the convergence between Clio and Themis but also of a crucial phase in the development of modern social thought.

La Thémis

> Empruntons à l'Allemagne ou plutôt reprenons-
> lui par droit de *postliminium*, cette excellente
> méthode historique empruntée de Cujas. . . .
> —Laboulaye (1839)

France was invaded by the historical school of law during the 1820s, and the principal vehicle was a remarkable journal, frankly modeled on and continuing the editorial line of Savigny's *Zeitschrift*. Called *La Thémis*, the journal was represented as a "library for the jurist" and brought out in 1819 in order to promote a renaissance of jurisprudence after the presumed dark age of the new French law since 1804.[1] It was sponsored by a distinguished international committee including Victor Cousin, Dupin, and Isambert, but the moving spirits were Athanase Jourdan and L. A. Warnkönig. Its purpose was not only to survey the history and teaching of law but also to invite critical reviews and discussions and to report on the progress of modern jurisprudence presented "in imitation of the jurists of Germany"; and its contributors included the greatest of European scholars from Niebuhr, Savigny, and Hugo on down. Savigny also gave the journal a favorable appreciation in his own periodical in 1820.

In the same year, *La Thémis* was joined by the Swiss publication *Annales de législation et de jurisprudence*, which had much the same form and goals and attracted equally impressive backing, including the historian Sismondi, Pelligrino Rossi, and Bentham's translator, Etienne Dumont. But after beginning with a flourish, this journal lapsed.[2] Although it commended the historical school, the Swiss *Annales* inclined less to a historical than to a philosophical mode, specifically political economy, a trend that the editors of *La Thémis* deplored.

After changing its name to *Annales de législation et d'économie politique*, the Swiss journal gave up the ghost (helped into its grave by Metternich's censorship) and delivered its mission wholly over to *La Thémis*, including a series of translations from Savigny's work. Rossi and Sismondi both migrated into what seemed to them the more promising field of economics.

Although *La Thémis* lasted barely a dozen years (its editor in chief, Jourdan, died in 1826 at the age of 35) and intermittently at that, its success was extraordinary. Jourdan wrote that, in 1804, no one would dream of publishing a serious history of Roman law (Dupin's was an elementary text), and for this reason indeed he turned his hand to translating Hugo's work. The first serious history of Roman law in French was by a contributor to *La Thémis*, Jacques Berriat-Saint-Prix, but he was just beginning to be affected by German scholarship. Rossi made the same criticism of it that Gans was to make of Savigny's: that it was not "internal" but merely "external" history.[3] In the 1820s, however, all this was changing. "No book published in Germany since Heineccius was known in Paris in 1819," Jourdan continued, while "in 1826 no code or other book that appears is neglected by *La Thémis*"—hence, he implied, not communicated to the French intellectual community.[4] In that same year, his journal listed over twenty German periodicals, antiquarian and professional, of significance to legal and historical scholarship. This portended another, if minor and marginal, "historical revolution."

In the work of these missionaries of the historical school, we can see not only the broadcasting of a controversial ideological message but also the making of a legend, for in his own day Savigny loomed as large on the European scene as did Guizot and Goethe (if not Hegel), and his teaching was more consistent and clearer, though (like Hegel's) adaptable to politics right or left. One of the first of the mythmakers was Warnkönig. His article in the first issue of *La Thémis* (1819) was a veritable *De l'Allemagne* of jurisprudence, declaring that Germany had given birth to a "new age of moral and political sciences" and that, after a preparatory interval from 1780 to 1790 including important works by Putter, Spittler, and especially Hugo, Savigny had taken over the leadership of this "revolution experienced over the past thirty years."[5] Jourdan waxed more philosophical over the consequences of this revolution and the international enterprise being carried on by *les jurisconsultes philosophes* of Europe. From this movement a "new philosophy" will arise, he predicted, and the "new direction of jurisprudence" will come from Plato.[6] Jourdan's profession of juridical faith appeared only posthumously, and it is unfortunately impossible to say just how he expected another neo-Platonism to direct and control the new philosophy he envisaged, though it must have involved some up-to-date incarnation of the old "spirit" of law.

The editorial views of *La Thémis* were seconded enthusiastically in the opening article of the Swiss *Annales*. Here Rossi dismissed the "dogmatic," "exegetic," and natural-law schools and argued that Savigny (rather than Thibaut) represented the truly "philosophical school of law."[7] For Rossi, Savigny's lesson was the value of historicism and, more important, of activism. "We live in a time of crisis for everything that concerns law and jurisprudence," wrote Rossi, referring to the aftermath of the revolutionary and codifying stages of social change. "This is the third reformation of the new social era," he continued, "the legislative reformation, less dangerous in its effects and more immediately useful than the political revolution, but it follows the same path and is the product of the same causes." Here was the lesson of history, for "since we are not men of the Middle Ages, we have an irresistible need to form for ourselves another jurisprudence and especially to avoid the obstacles to its natural development." In Rossi's view, the partnership between Clio and Themis was a condition of the "social revolution." Perhaps Jourdan had some such goal in mind, too, with the Platonic philosopher's returning to the cave being equivalent to the jurist's descending to social activism.

But the more immediate aims of *La Thémis* were practical

and by no means revolutionary. Professional periodicals, the *jurisprudence des arrêts*, collection of pleas, and especially the jurisprudence of the Civil Code were surveyed and criticized, as were law courses, taught abroad (Heidelberg, for example, and "Oxfort") as well as in France. The pedagogical value of history was celebrated as standing in the same relation to law as the "positive" method did to natural science, and again this was an indication of German influence. In the first course taught in legal history in Restoration Paris (1820), Professor Poncelet used German texts, notably that of Hugo.[8] One central professional issue in legal education, as in practical jurisprudence, was the utility of Roman law, especially with the growing body of indigenous jurisprudence. Ducaurroy urged that such courses at least be taught in French, but it was a struggle to maintain this subject as interest shifted to the sources of French law and to such specialties as commercial law.[9] These changes, too, were reflected in the pages of *La Thémis*.

Yet historical scholarship continued to dominate the journal. Ancient history was represented by publication of the report to the Berlin academy of the reconstruction of Gaius' *Institutes*; medieval history was represented by discussion of, for example, critical work on the *Establishments of Saint Louis* and the *Assizes of Jerusalem*; and modern history, by the seminal period of French jurisprudence in the sixteenth century, whose major figures were indeed the precursors of Savigny and his colleagues.[10] *Jurisprudentia Cujaciana* was the true ancestor of the *Historische Rechtsschule*, as various contributors to *La Thémis* were happy to recall.[11] Berriat-Saint-Prix not only began publishing the results of his critical study of Cujas in this journal but had the temerity to engage in public debates with elder German scholars on this subject. With Hugo he disputed the dating of a letter, and with Savigny the truth behind an amusing but unsavory episode in the career of Cujas at the University of Bourges.[12] (Did or did not Cujas, with the help of his student Pierre Pithou, climb into a religious house to abduct a certain *soeur augustine*? With hagiographic reasoning Berriat-Saint-Prix preferred to conclude not, while

Savigny, reviewing the legal evidence, considered it to be at least a possibility.) In a later dispute with another German scholar, F. A. Biener, Berriat-Saint-Prix defended Cujas against another charge, that he had mutilated a manuscript copy of Justinian's *Basilics*.[13] Not only Cujas but other "too neglected" jurists of that golden age were celebrated. Dupin in particular sang the praises of Pasquier, Loisel, Dumoulin, Ayrault, Bodin, and others as the founders of the grand tradition of modern jurisprudence, whose leadership had passed, at least temporarily, to Germany.[14] "Despite the distance of centuries," wrote one historian, "Hugo and Savigny are the disciples of Cujas and Doneau."[15] As another French admirer of the historical school later wrote, "Let us take over from Germany, or rather recover from exile there, that excellent historical method taken over from Cujas."[16]

La Thémis continued its international coverage of foreign periodicals and books. England was represented by discussions of Jeremy Bentham's widely disseminated pleas for a code of laws, antagonistic as it was to Savigny's doctrines, and of Henry Hallam's survey of medieval European literature; and Italy was represented by notices of Gravina's history of Roman law and especially of Vico's work on universal law preliminary to the *New Science*, which was becoming fashionable in the 1820s.[17] But as always, German interests predominated, and members of the historical school apparently had a standing invitation to express their views in the French journal. In response to Warnkönig's article, Hugo protested that the revival of legal studies had actually begun in 1789 rather than 1780, since 1789 had been the date of the first volume of his "course." Jourdan replied that it must have been a misprint.[18] Much attention was given to the work of Hugo, Thibaut, Niebuhr, and, endlessly, Savigny, most conspicuously through a summary of his great treatise on the law of possession, which was to have so significant an impact on French legal thought—and which illustrated as well the intimate ties between the historical school and sixteenth-century French scholarship.[19]

In the spirit of historicism, contributors to *La Thémis* showed the widest range of curiosity about the past, especially about the most mysterious and inaccessible aspect, including the law of the Twelve Tables and "the state of the Gauls at the time of the Frankish conquest."[20] Historical curiosity descended also to a miscellaneous sort of antiquarianism that today might be graced with the designation of popular culture or historical anthropology. The best example of this is the amusing controversy started by Berriat-Saint-Prix, when he published his findings about various attempts to bring legal proceedings against animals in the Old Regime. From the fifteenth century jurist Guy Pape, he reported the case of a pig that (who?) was hung (hanged?) in Châlons for an unnamed offense, and another case of a mule burned after his master for an offense that was named (though Berriat-Saint-Prix could not bring himself to repeat it).[21] In the next century, when the rat population of Mérindole (a town famous for the massacre of Protestants in 1540) threatened to get out of hand, the town authorities had the rats excommunicated—but not before appointing as their counsel the great jurist Barthélemy de Chasseneux. His *consilium* on this affair (fascinatingly consonant with his masterwork of 1529, *The Catalogue of the Glories of the World*, which discussed both nature and society in hierarchical terms) considered arguments about just how far one could go down the great chain of being into the animal world (insects? he speculated) and still expect "personal" responsibility. A third correspondent wrote to protest against taking such beliefs too lightly. If "our fathers" had chosen to believe in the personality of animals, that they in a sense had souls, what modern man at this space of time and secularism could say they were wrong? This might seem to be an admirable (if a touch facetious) attitude for a journal that opposed anachronism in all forms and claimed to celebrate the historical spirit.

In the fiercest tradition of Restoration journalism, *La Thémis* also kept the fires of controversy astir by critical and sometimes hypercritical reviews. One primary target was Guizot, who was attacked both for his translation of Gibbon, which Ducaurroy found uninformed by the law, and for his history of civilization, which Jourdan found superficial, ignorant of French as well as German scholarship, and suspiciously dependent on the work of others, especially the curious old assemblage of erudition by Mlle de Lézardière (whose book of 1792 Guizot had succeeded in getting republished).[22] Another scholar rebuked for being behind the times was the old *doyen* Toullier, who was attacked by Duranton and Demante (speaking on behalf of his old mentor Delvincourt) on grounds of academic rivalry and by Warnkönig for his failure even to mention Gaius.[23] Perhaps the most vitriolic critic was Lerminier's mentor Ducaurroy (writing sometimes as "A.T.H."), who was apparently an even worse tyrant in the classroom. What Ducaurroy could not stand was history without a foundation in the law. He tore apart an inept edition of the works of Cujas and deplored the lack of legal expertise in Gibbon as well as Guizot (Warnkönig came to Gibbon's rescue on the grounds that his professional failings may be counterbalanced somewhat by his "grandeur").[24] Almost a quarter-century after his attack on Guizot and Gibbon, Ducaurroy was still at it, quoting his early self in order to make the same charge against Laferrière and, by association, Lerminier's successor at the Collège de France, Laboulaye, adding for good measure sarcastic comments about the worthlessness of foreign honorary degrees (Laferrière had just received one from Tübingen).[25]

In general, what the *équipe* of *La Thémis* proposed to do by promoting "Germanism" was nothing less than to transform French jurisprudence and to make it a vehicle of social thought and social policy. It was applauded widely, even by the more popular press, though the writer for the *Globe* thought "it had a rather academic tone." The journal's influence extended through the 1820s; it trailed off after 1826, however, when Jourdan died, and it was then taken over from Liège by Warnkönig, who wrote an appreciation of Jourdan for Savigny's *Zeitschrift*.[26] *La Thémis* was the first of the great French legal history journals, and it served as a model for several successors, including the *Revue Foelix*, which began in 1834, the *Revue Wolowski*, in 1835, and finally the *Revue de législation*

91

et de jurisprudence, in 1851.[27] They are among the more important and most neglected vehicles of historical scholarship—and agents of the convergence of Clio and Themis—in the first half of the nineteenth century.

La Thémis constituted one of the most significant bridges between both French and German culture and history and law. Yet its emphasis, like Savigny's, remained professional. The first aim of the alliance between Clio and Themis was to prepare the way for a mature jurisprudence. History made it possible to formulate well-founded interpretations and judgments in keeping with social traditions and, as Savigny urged, to maintain "a lively connection with the primitive state of a people."[28] Other members of the historical school were not so backward-looking, but they agreed that historical perspective was essential for any substantial legal or social reforms. Arguably, such attitudes were almost inextricable from social and perhaps political conservatism; but there was a more curious and in many ways more enduring consequence, the impetus to antiquarian research on a grand scale. A whole dimension of investigation, a whole tradition of historical scholarship, spanning at least the past century and two-thirds, arose from the legal uses of history advertised in the pages of *La Thémis*.

A *Pléiade* of Legal Historians

> Il faut, pour comprendre le droit français,
> remonter au droit romain.
>
> —Portalis

By the 1830s the impact of the German historical school was abundantly apparent, not only in historical scholarship but also in professional jurisprudence, for instance in the work of such later commentators on the Code as J.L.E. Ortolan and R. T. Troplong. Also apparent, at least marginally, was the impact of Vico. By then the "new history," too, was well established. The members of Michelet's *pléiade* had accomplished most of their important work; four of them—Guizot, Thiers, Mignet, and Barante—had moved from scholarship to political activism, while Thierry was engaged from 1836 in collecting the sources of the history of the Third Estate as a sort of social hagiography (or martyrology) of the July Monarchy.[1] In the same decade other historians, working on a lower (and perhaps deeper) level, were busy examining the inheritance of law and jurisprudence as a way of understanding the process of national and European history, social and cultural as well as institutional and legal. To illustrate this juridical dimension of the new history, I introduce another five-member *pléiade*, comparable in scholarly significance if not in literary magnitude to Michelet's group. Each of these scholars also had, by no accident, a link with the German historical school and with the legal profession; each were devotees of both Clio and Themis.

Jean-Marie Pardessus (1772–1853) was really a member of the older generation, a traditionalist like Merlin, Henrion de Pansey, and Dupin who exhibited standards of scholarship perhaps not quite up to those of the historical school. His first published work, a treatise on agrarian servitudes and services, was devoted to a comparative study of Old Regime and modern law, hence in the most concrete terms to the historical process as reflected in legal sources.[2] His career had a practical as well as an academic side. He served first as a member of the imperial Corps Législatif and then as first professor of commercial law in the chair established by Napoleon in 1810. During the Restoration Pardessus was elected to the Chamber of Deputies and wrote extensively on commercial and maritime law, on which he assembled and published the first documentary collections, contributing also to the section on this subject in Dupin's *Profession of Advocate*.[3] His attachments to Old Regime mentality can be seen not only in his political inclinations but also in his later scholarship, including his edition of D'Aguesseau (1819) and especially in his continuation and termination of the collection of ordinances begun more than a century earlier by DuLaurier.[4]

Pardessus recognized that time and "the spirit of codification" had rendered largely obsolete many institutions of the Old Regime, but he continued to insist on their historical value and turned his attention to the seminal period of feudal custom, taking up where the old Académie des Inscriptions had left off in 1791.[5] In 1829 *La Thémis* welcomed into its pages his report on the *Assizes of Jerusalem*. After the revolution of 1830 sent him into permanent scholarly exile, Pardessus was able to concentrate fully on medieval law, most notably in editing Merovingian documents and the devilishly difficult text of the Salian Law. Though more a devotee of old legal traditions than of modern historicism, he received an exceptional stamp of approval from the historical school. He deserves a place, though he has not really found one, among the fathers of nineteenth-century "scientific" history.

Louis-Firmin-Julien Laferrière (1798–1861) belongs more properly to the generation of Restoration scholars.[6] He, like Pardessus, was a practicing lawyer and statesman as well as a professor of law. He taught at the University of Rennes, became inspector general of the faculty of law in 1846, and held a number of administrative offices during the Second Empire; he was also a founder of two journals, the *Revue de législation et de jurisprudence* and the *Revue historique de droit français et étranger*. His scholarly reputation derived from the pioneering history of French law that he first published in 1836 and later combined with his study of ancient law, taking the view of Portalis that "to understand French law it is necessary to go back to Roman law."[7] The need for this was not merely the "reason" embedded in civil law but, as Savigny had argued for Germany, the developmental connections between it and French traditions, especially from the sixteenth century. That this view was more than an antiquarian genuflection is also shown in Laferrière's interpretative study, virtually an *esprit des lois*, he boasted, of revolutionary legislation and the succeeding *droit intermédiaire*.[8]

Laferrière was also familiar with the work of the German historical school and its remote French predecessors and, through Michelet, with the "symbolism" of Creuzer and the historicism of Vico. He rejected the view of Vico (and the similar one of Niebuhr) that Roman law, far from producing feudal law, had emerged from its own "feudal" state; but in a general, if more eclectic, fashion he was in sympathy with their conception of law as a unique product of national development. On various grounds Laferrière's scholarship was questioned by both jurists and historians, among them Ducaurroy, Warnkönig, Klimrath, and Mittermaier.[9] But he continued to improve and augment his book in later editions, and he merits more attention than he has received as a pioneer of modern historical scholarship.

A more critical and more highly regarded historian of Roman law was Charles-Joseph-Barthélemy Giraud (1802–1881), another founder of the *Revue de législation et de jurisprudence*, who studied and after 1839 taught law at the University of Aix.[10] In 1842 Giraud became inspector-general of legal education until being succeeded by Laferrière, and held other academic posts until his appointment as professor of law in

95

Paris during the Second Empire. He felt a certain collegiality with practitioners of the contemporary "new history," but deplored the ignorance of law displayed by Guizot and Thierry. In 1835 he wrote an introduction to the translation of Heineccius' old manual and later published it separately as an up-to-date history of Roman law. In 1838 he also published (and dedicated to Thiers) a fundamental monograph on the Roman law of property that raised an issue crucial to both the German historical school and the July Monarchy.[11] Though familiar with the current giants of historical interpretation (Vico and Niebuhr as well as Hugo and Savigny), Giraud was inclined to give more credit to Cujas, Doneau, and company; and like many of those members of the first historical school of law, he turned from ancient to modern, from Roman to French, concerns.

Giraud's national focus appeared particularly in his study of medieval law and in his essay on Etienne Pasquier. Giraud celebrated the whole legist tradition, including Claude de Seyssel, François Hotman, Jean Du Tillet, Charles Dumoulin, and Pothier; but he identified more directly with Pasquier, who was historian as well as jurist, feudist as well as civilian.[12] The parallel between the two is striking: both started out from the *barreau*, which in Giraud's words "issued from that great and strong bourgeoise daughter of our universities and fathered by our old parlementary nobility," both were political loyalists devoted to the study of national tradition, and both took a comparative approach to legal history. As the "Cujacian" Pasquier followed the order of Justinian's *Institutes* in his study of medieval law, so Giraud followed that of Napoleon's Romanoid Code. In many of their values and specific judgments, they seem to be colleagues carrying out the same professional and scholarly enterprise. The parallel, and the affiliation, was not lost upon Sainte-Beuve in his review of Pasquier's *Interpretation of the Institutes of Justinian*, published for the first time in 1847 and preceded by Giraud's learned and hagiographical biographical notice. The common denominator was, in antiquarian and ideological terms, a boundless "respect for law."

Edouard-René-Lefebvre de Laboulaye (1811–1883) was trained as an advocate, and his interests were also more scholarly than practical.[13] Like Lerminier, whom he succeeded as professor of comparative legislation in the Collège de France, Laboulaye had studied in Germany. Indeed, he was regarded by Lord Acton as the only worthy disciple of Savigny in France. As a publicist for this historical school, he was more faithful, if not more active, than Lerminier. He was conscious of his isolation and attached little importance to "precursors." "The eighteenth century had broken sharply with the past," he declared, and the damage did not begin to be repaired until 1814 in Germany.[14] In France a small phalanx, mostly foreign, began to introduce the new jurisprudence, but fifteen years later the task had still not been accomplished. Scholarship in the *magistrature*, except for that of Pardessus, was "dogmatic" rather than historical. Among commentators on the Code, only Troplong brought to bear historical criticism and some knowledge of the work of Guizot and Thierry.

During the 1840s Laboulaye continued to broadcast the message of the historical school, especially in his laudatory biography of Savigny and in his pioneering study of property law in western civilization, a book that drew together many of the themes of the French tradition and the German movement.[15] His campaign was directed in particular at the reform of legal education, which he proposed to broaden not only through history but also through comparative law, philosophy, and political economy. Only in this way, Savigny had taught, could jurisprudence be brought up to a level on which a legal system could be seriously contemplated.[16] In later years he carried on his mission as chief editor of the greatest of the successors to *La Thémis*, the *Revue historique de droit français et étranger*, which has been published continuously since 1855. The range of Laboulaye's later work was truly extraordinary, especially in the area of comparative law, and it included American and women's history. His significance derived originally, however, from his labors as the most devoted alumnus of the German historical school.

The brightest hope of this generation of historians was undoubtedly Henri Klimrath (1807–1837), who (according to Laboulaye) would have given France both her Savigny and her Eichhorn; that is, he would have been both her leading Romanist and her leading Germanist.[17] Klimrath was also the one who had enjoyed the most substantial contacts with German scholarship, having studied with Thibaut, Stahl, Zachariae, Mittermaier, and Schlosser, among others. Like his *paysan* Lerminier, he was something of a prodigy, receiving his doctorate of law from the University of Strasbourg in 1833 and assuming the chair of law the following year. A partisan of the historical school from 1829, he wrote on practical as well as antiquarian subjects, on the value of history for the interpretation of the Code as well as monographic studies of medieval customs and legislation.[18] Klimrath did not take as dim a view of the state of French scholarship as Laboulaye or Savigny had, and he singled out Portalis and Merlin in particular for praise. But he deplored the absence of law in the new history of Guizot and Thierry, he shared Laboulaye's suspicions of the poetical excesses of Michelet, and he found that even the work of Laferrière "left something to be desired" (specifically, the "internal dimension" of legal history).[19]

Klimrath had a conceptual as well as a "scientific" and professional interest in the historical process, especially in the problem of sudden change, whether through revolution or through codification. Here he was following the line of thought of Portalis and the redactors, and of course entering into the problems of legal interpretation. He opposed the notion of the constancy of human nature and of uniform and unilinear causation, and he turned his attention to questions of social divergence and diversity. And like Laferrière, Klimrath was not content with the simple analysis of legal texts. Without going as far as Michelet in symbolistic and "poetic" divination, he was persuaded that institutions and social patterns long antedated, and had to be reconstructed from such texts

as, say, those of feudal law. He was thus led to his fundamental interest in local customs. His plan, retracing the steps
of Dumoulin three centuries before, was to survey all of the
provincial *coutumes* of France according to their geographic and
historical singularity in order to reconstitute the national tradition of French law.[20] His primary aim, in other words, was
not the learned jurisprudence studied by Savigny but rather
that first and less accessible variety that Savigny had referred
to as the "aggregate existence of the community": the *Volksgeist*, as reflected in historical monuments in the most concrete
and positive ways.

Klimrath wanted to be a social historian in the most comprehensive sense, and yet he remained ever the professional
jurist. In his assault on customary law in particular we can
see the perfect union of scholarly and practical motives in the
French historical school. This was expressed perhaps most
clearly in Klimrath's hermeneutical formula of "historical equity" (*l'équité historique*), without which law would be "capri-
cious and arbitrary." The basic condition of this historical
equity was the principle that modern law had to be interpreted in the light of social usages; and in support of this
Klimrath invoked the famous Roman maxim, neatly convey-
ing the view of Savigny as well, that "custom is the best interpreter of law" (*Optimum enim est legum interpres consuetudo*).
Thus a history of French law would have both "a scientific
and a social importance." Unfortunately, Klimrath died at the
age of thirty; his work, barely launched, was published posthumously by Warnkönig, former editor of *La Thémis*, just before Warnkönig's own death.

Fundamental and groundbreaking as they were, the accomplishments of this group have not been appreciated on the
level of either science or society.[21] Historiographically, they
were of course overshadowed by the more popular creations
of Michelet and his *pléiade*, and they were virtually submerged
by the more critical and comprehensive labors of the aggres-
sively "scientific" historians of the latter part of the century
(who had their own "social" concerns and were under a sim-

ilar debt to German scholarship). Yet without their example and preliminary labors, the accomplishments of later nineteenth-century medievalists such as Fustel de Coulanges, Viollet, Esmein, Glasson, Chenon, Tardif, and Arbois de Jubainville would hardly have been possible. It may be an exaggeration to regard these later scholars as dwarves on the shoulders of giants, or humdrum settlers following the real mountain men (if only because sixteenth-century medievalists were the true pioneers); but they were abundantly endowed beneficiaries of a great generation of historical science that preserved and extended a long tradition of scholarship.

CHAPTER NINE

Michelet and the Law

> L'humanité est son oeuvre à elle-même.
> —Vico (1725); Michelet (1827)

In reach if not in grasp, Michelet surpassed both this *pléiade* and the one defined by himself. He was a true product of 1830—indeed he found his ideological identity in that revolution and proclaimed that history in general would be an "eternal July."[1] For the *trois Glorieuses* signified the victory of "liberty" over "fatalism" and the basis of that "resurrection" of the French past that had become his life's obsession. By this time, Michelet had already served his apprenticeship and was emerging as the leading practitioner of the "new history" established in the previous decade. In addition to his teaching at the Ecole Normale, he had published a best-selling textbook of modern history and his translation of Vico.[2] He had also made important inroads into German scholarship, especially (through Quinet) Herder's studies of popular culture, Niebuhr's reconstructions of prehistorical Rome, Creuzer's "symbolic" theories of myth, Jakob Grimm's "poetry of law," and other products of the historical school. In 1828 he made his first scholarly *iter* across the Rhine and had entered into a fruitful correspondence with Grimm.[3] At the same time, he was listening to the famous lectures of Guizot, reading Thierry's manifestos of the new history, and lamenting the "fatalism" of both (as well as devouring Romantic poetry and novels). Through his readings of Grimm, Eichhorn, Mittermaier, and Gans and of Roman history, he was attracted increasingly to the law, which in fact he had begun studying as early as 1820.

In the fall of 1829 Michelet was able for the first time to

101

devote all of his teaching to history, and so he plunged into the problem of the origins of Rome, making extensive use of Niebuhr but not hesitating to register disagreements and his own even riskier speculations. As both Niebuhr and Vico had taught, the Roman law of the Twelve Tables represented the oldest and clearest expression of "poetic wisdom." It was precisely during Michelet's lectures on this monument and on the social conflict of patricians and plebeians reflected in it that the revolution broke out on the streets of Paris, replicating in a way the Roman expulsion of the Etruscan kings of Rome (the subject of his lecture just two weeks before).[4] It was Tuesday, 27 July: the *Globe*, the *National*, and *Le Temps* had appeared despite government prohibition; Guizot, Thiers, and Mignet were busy writing pro-Orleanist manifestos; the crowds had gathered in the afternoon; and around three o'clock the first insurgent was killed. The following Tuesday, 3 August, when Michelet finished his discussion of the Twelve Tables in his last scheduled lecture, the Duke of Orleans announced the abdication of Charles X. So dawned, for Michelet and many others, the vision of "eternal July," the final victory of the "people" (Michelet's translation of plebeian) over the aristocracy.

But the key to Michelet's efforts of "reconstruction" was Vico's "new science," which he not only read and translated but also, in his own work, transmuted. Here was the true "internal history" not merely of law, though that was its base, but of humanity in general. In Restoration France, Vico was in a sense waiting to be discovered, though his work had been known to de Maistre, Fauriel, Degérando, and Cousin, among others. In 1817 Guizot tried to get Fauriel to write an article on Vico for the short-lived *Archives Philosophiques*, and Pierre Ballanche published Vico's seminal essay on "the most ancient wisdom of the Italians." In fact, there was allegedly a translation of the *New Science* in progress when Michelet announced his own version in the pages of *La Thémis*.[5] For Cousin, who had encouraged Michelet's project, this book was "the model and perhaps the source of the *Spirit of the Laws*," though it seemed to him inferior to the even wider-reaching work of Herder, the translation of which he had assigned to Quinet.[6] Michelet became the apostle of Vichianism in France, and it informed much of his work on French as well as ancient history. Through the "new science," he hoped, the "new history" could fulfill the ideal of nineteenth-century historicism and become a true "philosophy of history."

Michelet's inspiration through Vico, an example of a sort of higher parasitism, suggests also a major link between Michelet's conception of history and the law. Vico's own point of departure had been jurisprudence, specifically the tradition of Roman law, which itself claimed to be identical with true wisdom—"the science of things divine and human," as Michelet once noted. Taking Roman experience as the principal historical archetype, Vichian methodology centered on the "axiom" that "the nature of institutions is nothing but their coming into being at certain times and in certain guises."[7] For Vico these origins meant "poetic wisdom," an aboriginal culture that was religious, mythical, and in a sense instinctual. The aim of the "new science" was to reconstruct this primitive state of mind through the earliest texts and language, especially etymology. What made historical understanding possible, indeed "scientific," was the underlying condition that what men had made themselves, they could grasp conceptually: the "made" and the "true" were the same thing, according to the famous Vichian formula *verum esse ipse factum*.[8] In Michelet's rendition, man makes himself: "L'humanité est son oeuvre à elle-même." By that he expressed both the basis of his heaven-storming intention to "divine" the human past and his faith in the ultimate identity of history and the story of human liberty. "Social science dates from the day," Michelet added, "when this great idea was expressed for the first time."

The history of law, which began in fact (*de facto, ex facto*) and ended in jurisprudence if not codification, illustrated the emergence of culture from "poetic wisdom." In the words of Justinian cited by both Vico and Michelet, Roman jurispru-

103

dence originated in "fables of ancient law" (*fabulae antiqui juris* indeed became the motto for Michelet's work in legal history).[9] For Vico, moreover, the oldest law, that of the Twelve Tables, was in fact a "serious poem" in the sense both that it had been chanted and that it represented the customs of a primitive mentality in a mythical stage of development. Similarly, Michelet called it a "terrible song of patrician domination."[10] As such poetic elements and antique formalisms showed, Roman law was founded on religion: *jus* emerged from *fas*. Michelet tried in his *Roman History* to retrace the Vichian *corso* from the "poetic" to the "heroic" down to the "human" stage of culture, though he had recourse also to the more scholarly efforts of Niebuhr to draw upon poetic sources. The primitive "poetic necessity of individualizing ideas" through symbol and personification made it possible to exhume the essential institutions of Roman civilization. A prime example of this is the sacred character of landed property, symbolized first in the cult of the god Terminus established by Numa and realized later in the sacred *ager Romanus*, possession of which was a special privilege of the patriciate. Of course proprietary ambitions were fulfilled on a larger scale in the mature ideology of the Empire, the "poetic" worship of land being transformed into a "heroic" drive for conquest and then the "human" institutions of political control.[11]

But to this Vichian cycle of legal history Michelet added his own special emphasis arising from the July-inspired theme of liberty versus "fatality."[12] Expelling the Etruscan kings, the Romans emerged from their mythical period with a cry of liberty—their religion being a sort of "Protestantism" reacting to Etruscan religiosity, Michelet suggested—but, increasingly, authoritarian behavior and institutions prevailed. Personal liberty was subordinated to property even in the Roman family, whose members were under the *dominium* of the father. Of course such materialism was even more conspicuous in Roman political institutions, and especially in the law. Unlike most historians, including Gibbon, Michelet agreed with Vico that in the "poetic wisdom" of the Twelve Tables there was hardly a touch of Greek influence, only a mixture of Roman customs drawn from different historical stages: "sacerdotal" barbarism, "heroic" aristocracy, and the revolutionary republic with its newly found, if very restricted, "liberty."[13] To some extent, indeed, the Tables displayed features of a "charter" extracted from the patricians by the plebeians, reflected especially in the famous formula of primitive socialism, "The good of the people is the supreme law" (*Salus populus suprema lex*). But such liberty was undermined by class conflict, the institutions of slavery, the work of Roman lawyers, and the drive to conquest and imperial social organization. For Michelet the Roman model was the classic expression of the triumph of "fatalism."

Here especially Germanism came to Michelet's assistance, through the views of Niebuhr, whose boast that "there have never been slaves in my country" Michelet quoted, and through contact with the German historical schools of language and law. Through his readings in medieval German poetry and in the legal and linguistic antiquities published by Grimm, Michelet was encouraged to move from the course of Roman history to the medieval *ricorso* of national or "gentile" tradition, that wider "world of nations," the historical counterpart of the *jus gentium* that defined the conceptual field of the "new science." German philology had opened up cultural horizons through its discovery—"resurrection"—of a larger Indo-European prehistory, at least in linguistic and mythical terms. Michelet was persuaded enough to proclaim India as the "womb of the world" and the starting point for the story of liberty, which later passed on to Persia, Greece, Judaism, and finally the Germanic tribes, which represented France's own national origins.[14]

French history itself, according to Michelet, was broadly speaking the story of a long cultural war between Romanism and Germanism—between "fatality" and "liberty," rationalism and symbolism, and perhaps even prose and poetry. In the texts of medieval French law there was unfortunately little poetry still remaining, for such primitive discourse, along with

105

personal liberty, had been overwhelmed by the prosaic influence of "written law" and by the royal courts, which had effaced the symbolism of the Frankish heritage. About this native legal wisdom Michelet wrote that "the Parlement [of Paris], great protector, translated, interpreted, and killed it."[15] It was against a similar legalism, one embodied in the papal curia, that Luther had struggled; and this phase of Germanic "liberty" Michelet also celebrated, in articles published in 1832. His immediate aim was to understand "the great revolution of the sixteenth century," he told Quinet in 1827, but beyond this and more fundamentally "to know the old German nationality, which is the source of this movement."[16] This was the pivotal point of Michelet's great *History of France*, which began to appear in 1833.

But for Michelet the "new history" was more than national self-adulation. It had become, he wrote the year before, "this elevated science that promises to explain the origins of human destinies." Through Germanism, in the form especially of (often fanciful) mythological theories of Creuzer and the linguistic archeology of Grimm, Michelet was led to expand his conception of the new science into a "symbolic" or "poetic of law." Since at least 1830 he had been playing with the notion of "the poetry of law and of agriculture."[17] His idea was that the movement, reflected in primal Roman experience, was from the "epic poetry" of agricultural society to the "dramatic poetry" of the period of law. Through Germanism, in other words, Michelet was led to his most Vichian book. In fact, it was a "general symbolic of law" or, as he also referred to it, "a concordance of barbaric, ecclesiastical, and feudal institutions."[18] But when it appeared in 1837, he preferred to call this, his most metahistorical effort of "resurrection," *The Origins of French Law*.

It is a puzzling work, lyrical rather than analytical; one in which Michelet selects, arranges, and evokes, but never explains. Had he found a new way of looking at antique literature, or was he, in Andre Chenier's famous phrase, making "ancient verses on new subjects"? It was surely "new," but was it history? It was extravagantly learned, making use of Old Regime as well as modern scholarship (including Du Cange and DuLaurier), but it was also intuitive to an extreme. It reached back for prehistory, but it often caught the contemporary. Behind the chains of illustrations drawn from that "Indian Digest," the *Laws of Manu*, and the "dramatic formalism" of Roman law to the intensely personal constructions of Germanic and feudal custom, the larger theme remained the encounters between liberty and fatality. Like other works of Michelet's, *The Origins of French Law* was autobiographical in a sense. It was "one of the grand passions of my life," he told his future son-in-law in 1841. "It was, I may say, life itself for a certain time."[19] Never before had there been such an intense effort to humanize legal history. Of laws and man Michelet sang, and he sang as a man or poet, not a legist. Human, too, was his principle of organization: a trajectory from cradle to grave, a "juridical biography of man," a sort of legalistic *Divine Comedy* (an analogy to which Vico had also appealed) appropriate to the Vichian principle that "ancient jurisprudence was poetic throughout."[20]

Michelet followed the time-honored order of civil law, at least since Gaius.[21] Personality, that first face of the Roman juridical trinity of persons, things, and actions, received first expression in the baby's cry; but it became institutionalized, or legal, only through reception into the family. For the Romans this passage out of a state of nature was accomplished by the will of the father, the alternative (for many primitive societies) being exposure and death. Reception into society was signaled by the "formula of milk or honey," that is, embracing by the mother, who serves the father and his potential heir.[22] This contrasted with the Germans, who accepted the child himself (or herself) and who derived the notion of property from the family rather than the reverse. Christianity added sanctification to respect through the universal water-symbolism of baptism, the first "social initiation." The second initiation—second birth, second communion—was marriage, which was likewise surrounded and expressed by symbols, notably

those of clothing, household arrangement, and gifts. Book I
of *The Origins* elaborates on the symbolism of family in eclectic and transhistorical terms, with reference to sources as disparate as the Hindu laws, Plutarch, Bracton, medieval poetry, Luther's *Table Talk*, and French provincial customs.

Book II treats another sort of union and set of symbolisms,
that between man and the land: "property" in all of its rich
and contradictory ambiguities. The institution of "property,"
preceded or perhaps supplemented by "occupation" and "possession," was the product of a sort of *confarreatio* (Roman marriage ceremony) between man and nature, which is in a sense
to say between freedom and necessity.[23] "This is my place in
the sun . . . ," Michelet quotes the proverb (not from Rousseau, he points out, but from Pascal). "Here is the origin of
the usurpation of the land," which is to say occupation. "The
place of a man, that which he can cover with his body, that
is the true measure of primitive property, . . . hardly more
than place for a tomb." And he adds the Vichian observation,
"Such is the infantile and profound thought of ancient times."
Whence, however, emerged a wealth, indeed a superabun-
dance, of proprietary concepts and symbols that, rationalized
and civilized, came to make up much of the substance of law.
"From equivocation to equivocation," Michelet remarked,
"property will slide over the whole earth."[24] The model was
the Roman *ager*, but it had counterparts in the Germanic *Mark*
("marked" land) and medieval allod (my "lot"). Property was
a social mystery, beginning as a simple and necessary love of
the soil and ending in gross territorial imperatives and "imperialism." Enthusiasts could identify it with God himself:
Fundus optimus maximus. Not only had property attracted symbols, especially boundary marks such as a stone or a spear, it
was itself richly symbolic and "in poetic ages appeared as a
person." As in feudal times it signified honor, so later it was
an embodiment of that Germanic liberty that was established
first by the English and then fulfilled by the French.

It is hardly possible to give in brief compass an adequate

notion of Michelet's ingenious, insightful, mystifying, mytho-
poeic, pedantic, and thoroughly self-indulgent experiment—
speculative history, Sismondi called it—except to say that it
is more Vichian than Vico (and for orthodox scholars grim-
mer than Grimm). Having dealt with the family and property, Michelet went on to topics of adult and public life, that
is, politics, war, and criminal law, and finally the end of the
private human *corso*, death and interment, again in terms of
symbolism and ceremonial. Like Vico he tended to regard
public law as an extension of private law, political arrangements as the effects of prescription and reason on custom,
and, in general, law as a product of necessity made virtuous
by authority. Governments were robber bands legitimized by
the attribution of symbols of justice and humanity, to reverse
the Augustinian formula; or in Vichian terms, governments
arose out of a primitive age dominated by "the law of private
violence." A man, aping the gods, becomes "king," enhanced
by symbols of worship and trappings of legitimacy; and the
pattern is repeated on all levels of society. Nature-, color-,
and number-symbolism, heraldic arms, and other inarticulate
expressions of social behavior—all represented a pre- or ex-
traverbal language that Michelet claimed to read and to interpret, at least tacitly.[25] So, too, with the forms and formulas
of feudal law, oaths and proofs, penalties and punishments,
and many less classifiable anecdotes and pieces of curious erudition, presented portentously, though usually without comment.

What did it all mean? Although he classified texts and symbols according to their place in the life cycle, Michelet seldom
tried to offer specific decipherment, and no doubt thereby
saved himself much criticism. As it was, contemporary reactions ranged from bewilderment to complaints that it was hardly
more than a translation of Grimm's work, from enthusiasm to
(usually professional) disapproval.[26] What precisely was a
symbol? Was it a license for "pure fantasy" (a historian's
"dream," as Heine suggested)[27] or obscurantism or (as Fré-

déric Ozanam feared) a means of undermining orthodox religion? Saint-Marc Girardin agreed with Michelet's emphasis on "the Germanic principle," but objected to his mysticism.[28] Henri Klimrath objected that Michelet had been too easily "seduced by all this poetry," forgetting that the "symbolic of law" was not law itself, while other jurists complained about Michelet's amateurish ignorance of the law in general.[29] *Optimus maximus* was a good civilian formula, for example, and the association of the Roman *confarreatio* with the occupation of land was too remote even for a symbol. Laferrière, on the other hand, who had just published his own *History of French Law*, praised Michelet's efforts as valuable for the philosophy both of law and of history, and so did the jurist Frédéric Taulier.[30] Laferrière appreciated in particular the way in which Michelet had depicted the growing up of humanity, and he expressed the hope that Michelet, having shown the "symbolic" of law, would now in his *History of France* show its "dialectic," that is, its movement.

The only reader of Michelet's book who may be regarded as in any way his disciple was J. P. Chassan, who in 1847 published an ambitious *Essay on the Symbolic of Law*, along with a discussion of "the poetry of primitive law," which also drew on the work of Vico, Creuzer, Grimm, and Ballanche and legal historians such as Laferrière and Beugnot. Chassan's purpose was to establish a classification of juridical symbolism from the natural symbols of mythical times down to the complex intellectual fictions of the modern age, ending with an analysis of the Civil Code. His assumption was that law was perhaps the most fundamental aspect of cultural history. "Formerly in Rome and still in modern societies," he wrote, "law is the greatest of the human sciences."[31]

The Origins of French Law, though one of the most impressive products of the nineteenth-century encounter between history and law, has had no great impact on either field, nor even on revived interest in Michelet. The author himself did not travel further down Vico's road. Instead he turned to more

110

familiar, and more French, subjects. In 1838 he was appointed both to the Institute of France and, as Daunou's successor, to the chair of history at the Collège de France, where he pursued more narrowly his life task of historical "resurrection." In 1846 he published an even more personal book, *The People*, to celebrate the mythical and mystical unity of France. "This book is more than a book, it is myself," he wrote in his dedication to his old comrade Quinet, with whom he had recently carried on a campaign against the Jesuits.[32] He had carried his history of France through the Middle Ages and was launching into his great history of the Revolution. He displayed an almost evangelical faith in the "destiny" that history revealed for France. A variety of "servitudes" remained, he argued, but social "classes" were obsolete, having been superseded by national differences, with France "noble" and the rest of Europe "plebeian." For the fears and hopes of socialists like Proudhon, he had nothing but contempt; nor did he think that jurisprudence was the key. "Were you Germans or Italians," he exhorted, "I would say to you, 'Consult the legists; you have only to follow the rules of civil equity.'— But you are France; you are not a nation only, you are . . . a great political principle."

This political principle was revolution, but Michelet was hardly prepared for the form it was to take two years after the publication of *The People* in 1846. "I define Revolution—," he wrote, "the advent of the law, the resurrection of Right, and the reaction of Justice." But what 1848 saw was rather the advent of the political and especially the "social." The truth is that, like Guizot, Michelet remained a man of 1830; like Guizot, he was toppled from his position of eminence (though not from literary popularity) and even historiographical authority. Yet while he gave history a new name, he did not "mark the end" of it, and his appeal of 1846 seems singularly ill-timed. "Frenchmen of all conditions, of all classes, remember this one thing: you have but one sure friend on this earth—France."[33] Hardly a year later, a similar sounding appeal would be sent out with the formula just reversed, to men of one class but of "all nations." The manifesto of Marx (who had been expelled from Paris early in 1845 by Guizot's order) was raised likewise on a rejection of traditional law. It marked both a new conception of society and a new view of "revolution"—in short, yet another "new history," though its context was still, in a sense, the intersection of history and law.

Between History and Reason

Un code est à la fois un système et une histoire.
—Lerminier (1831)

What has been called "the German mirage" fascinated some members of the post-Napoleonic generation, but it repelled many others. This foreign influence had reached the highest echelons of the legal profession in France, reflected, for example, in the last edition of Camus' *Profession of Advocate* (1832). The *Revue encyclopédique* charged Dupin with "encouraging a small sect that is trying to introduce Germanism into jurisprudence," especially in the university. Dupin responded by distinguishing erudition from conceptualization. "One can compare the Germans to laborers adept at quarrying stone," he wrote. "In this sort of work, that of research, of patient and laborious erudition, they have a real and sometimes superior merit; but in building and regular construction one must recognize their inferiority to the French."[1] This was an attitude common to professionals, who hoped to protect the "principles of French jurisprudence" from foreign invasions.[2]

On the academic side, however, "Germanism" had indeed made its way into legal thinking. The best example of this was young Strasbourgeois Eugène Lerminier, who studied with Ducaurroy in the faculty of law and who made his journalistic debut with an article on Montesquieu for *La Thémis*. Lerminier's career was remarkable, and it all started with jurisprudence. In 1826 he was already reviewing for the *Globe*, praising the "new science" extracted from history by Vico and Montesquieu, while carrying on his own search for a "true science at once rational and historical."[3] The following year he published his Latin thesis on Savigny's great treatise on

113

the Roman law of possession, recently summarized by Warn-könig in the pages of *La Thémis*.[4] The next year Lerminier opened his extraordinarily popular course of lectures and be-gan spreading the word of the historical school of law both in his teaching (at the Collège de France after 1830) and in a stream of publications, articles for popular journals such as the *Revue des deux mondes*, and books. During an incredibly prolific decade Lerminier moved eclectically from jurispru-dence into other areas of philosophy, literature, and politics, experimenting with Saint-Simonianism in his search for a modern "social science," but drawing his inspiration above all from "beyond the Rhine." In a sense a political counterpart of his fellow Saint-Simonian Sainte-Beuve, Lerminier also be-came the self-proclaimed successor of Mme de Staël as the apostle of Germanism in France, most notably in his collec-tion of essays published in 1835 as *Au delà du Rhin*.

For Lerminier the "German impulse" had begun centuries before. By throwing off Roman hegemony, he wrote, the Germans had begun modern history, and from the time of the Revolution the French were carrying the German idea of freedom into the political and social spheres.[5] He praised con-temporary German achievements in the fields of philosophy, philology, history, and especially legal scholarship. He re-peated the received wisdom that sixteenth-century French jurisprudence had prepared the way for Savigny, and he sang the praises of Cujas (foolishly, some critics thought) as one who "had loved Roman law as a Romantic poet and had cul-tivated it as an artist."[6] On such a basis, in any case, Lermi-nier built up an historical reconstruction of a philosophy of law that would combine Enlightenment theory and values with nineteenth-century "legislation and sociability." Like Rossi, Hello, and other discriminating admirers of the German his-torical school, Lerminier hoped to continue the "revolution" in a more legitimate fashion through a new social philosophy derived from jurisprudence. In a sense, he was an old-fash-ioned *philosophe* in a nineteenth-century context.

While taking Savigny's brand of historicism as his point of

departure, Lerminier was also aware of the criticisms lodged against it—not only by defenders of French rationalism but also by proponents of German idealism. "At the present time," wrote Lerminier in 1829, "the historical school and the new philosophical school are represented at [the University of] Berlin by Savigny and M. [Eduard] Gans. The war is spectacular. In the historical school they are afraid of philosophy. . . . In the philosophical camp they look down with pity on the purely historical jurists."[7] Lerminier would not go as far as Marx in rejecting jurisprudence altogether, but he did agree about the passivity of historicism: the tendency to identify historical fact with juridical ideal. The upshot of uncritical historicism would be to "abandon the legality of a country to its instincts," argued Lerminier in 1831. It was "to misunderstand the office of social science," he continued, "to set jurisprudence above legislation, technical procedures above life itself, erudition above philosophy, the past above the present, and ancient usages and customs about the modern spirit, and to surrender the initiative of reason."[8] All this sounded too much like the Ultra view, expressed by Bonald, that "a society tends to perfect its law as a river to correct its course."

The initiative of reason was still powerful in the French legal profession, and it was reinforced by the German philosophical school. This was especially clear in the field of legal hermeneutics, attached as it was to the Civil Code and its conventions. All commentators on the Code had a section on "how to interpret the laws," and their discussions as a rule were utterly conventional, differing little from those of their medieval professional forebears. Interpretation had to be both historical and rational, since the facts of a case had to be determined before the relevant law and since the intention of the legislator had to be decided before introducing questions of equity. "It is the will of the legislator that constitutes law," wrote Demante, "but this will is always determined by a principle of eternal justice or by a motive of particular utility."[9] Yet this determination should not be surrendered merely to judicial will, and beyond this premise jurists went into sup-

115

plementary sources of interpretation, especially custom and precedent. It was here that historicism had at least a marginal impact, since appeal to such sources introduced elements of relativism that, according to a minority view, might even improve the equitability of interpretation. This seems to be what Henri Klimrath had in mind when, in the context of his antiquarian investigations, he spoke of "historical equity."[10] Even Klimrath, however, assumed that history was a way not to modify universal standards but only to make them more concrete and adaptable to social reality.

In 1822 Mailher de Chassat, a translator of Thibaut's influential book on interpretation, published his own more systematic treatise on the subject as an introduction to "the new French law."[11] Mailher associated modern jurisprudence with the grand traditions of natural science: the empirical tradition of Bacon and Locke, the rationalist tradition of Leibniz and Descartes, and especially the tradition of those whom Savigny called the "systematists," including Le Douaren, Doneau, Domat, and Pothier. Mailher tried to join the particular with the universal, and (for himself as well as for Thibaut) he denied that history had been neglected. The "science of law" had three parts: "didactics" (research and exposition), history, and exegesis; and "history," according to the distinction made by Leibniz and made famous by Hugo, was both "external" and "internal," that is, construed in terms both of its sources and of its inner logic.[12] For Mailher the sources included Roman and customary law, the *jurisprudence des arrêts*, canon and feudal law, legal authorities, and modern legislation. This massive historical legacy was the basis for the "system of rules called the hermeneutics of law" (*herméneutique du droit*), a "scientific method" leading from philology to philosophy and from particular cases to general principles. Such was the French view of the "philosophical school of law."

French intellectuals of various persuasions shared the rationalistic proclivities of Mailher and his suspicions of the excesses of historicism. From the right and left respectively, Chateaubriand and Michelet complained of the "fatalism" of the historical school and some of its French followers, while even Guizot, under the same charge, objected to certain implications of Savigny's conception, which seemed to subordinate the vitality and the color of history to its "anatomy" and "physiology."[13] In part, Guizot was making a plea for narrative historiography, but even more, he was arguing for a view of history that accommodated change in the future as well as in the past, which in general was to say bourgeois "progress." This was of course in keeping with lawyers, who wanted to build for the future on the foundations laid in the Code and in its orthodox commentators. The impact of the philosophical school was apparent in many professional publications, including the enormously successful textbook by Aubry and Rau (first edition 1834), actually a reordered translation of K. S. Zachariae's old handbook of the Code (first edition 1808), and in J. F. Taulier's work devoted to a "reasoned theory of the Code," which was innocent not only of foreign influence but also of legal history, including Roman law, Old Regime law, and modern jurisprudence.[14]

But this approach also represented an extreme. What most French jurists preferred was a balance between historicism and rationalism. The moderate position was illustrated perhaps most clearly by Alexandre Ledru-Rollin, who was Lerminier's collaborator on the journal *Le Droit* and likewise a critic of the alleged or potential obscurantism and especially the "fatalism" of Savigny and French disciples like Laboulaye. This "exotic baggage" from *outre-Rhin* was pedantry without political value. Writing for the oldest of all professional legal periodicals, the *Journal du palais*, Ledru-Rollin characterized the doctrine of the historical school in this way: "Law is not invented, it exists by itself, has roots in the body of the nation, grows and develops with it through its internal force. It is a necessary and determining element of the vast organism, and it should follow all the phases of the body's life. Men cannot legitimately tamper with it, for it would be contrary to nature to submit it to the tyranny of reason."[15] Nor was the pure reason of Hegel and Gans adequate for the science

117

of law. Instead, Ledru-Rollin invoked the ancient formula of Ulpian in the *Digest* identifying jurisprudence with true wisdom, "the knowledge of things divine and human" (*notitia rerum divinarum ac humanarum*), associating this with the Eclecticism of Cousin and Lerminier. "It is evident that each of these two schools has only a part of the truth," Ledru-Rollin wrote of the respective followings of Savigny and Gans. "One takes account only of the human element, the other only of the eternal divine; one sees only the contingent, the other only the necessary and absolute." French jurisprudence, he concluded, ought to attend to both parts of the formula: to both philosophy and human experience.

Yet in a sense this is what Savigny had been preaching all along; and as Thibaut could deny having neglected history, so Savigny could deny overlooking philosophy. Among French jurists his reputation continued to grow in the second quarter of the nineteenth century, especially because of the French translation by Charles Guenoux of his great history of Roman law in the Middle Ages (1839) and the laudatory biographical study by Edouard Laboulaye (1842). Mignet even urged that Savigny was, though German by birth, French by blood.[16] Savigny had never opposed codification as such, let alone philosophy, these interpreters argued. He had merely pointed out how premature and unhistorical such efforts were in the intellectual climate of post-Napoleonic Germany and, perhaps especially, France. Savigny himself, a practicing jurist, was actively involved in the reform of the Prussian *Landrecht*. Moreover, in 1840 he began publishing his own monumental contribution to systematic and "philosophical" jurisprudence, including a systematic discussion of legal hermeneutics. From Savigny's perspective, then, there was no conflict between history and philosophy—or for that matter between theory and practice.

Other French jurists, perhaps most of them, inclined to a narrower—a more national and *ad hoc*—approach that approximated what the Germans and English (though not the French) would later term "legal positivism." This was the at least tacit premise of the great collections of practical jurisprudence (cases, *arrêts*, and academic opinions) such as those of Merlin and of Devilleneuve and Gilbert, and of treatises such as Boulages' *Principles of French Jurisprudence*, which more or less consciously avoided non-French traditions. It was the articulated premise of perhaps the greatest jurist of the July Monarchy and successor to Henrion as Premier Président of the Cour de Cassation, Raymond Troplong (for whom, unlike Cujas and Toullier, there was unfortunately no street in Paris named). Troplong was quite familiar with the historical school, but believed that Savigny's work was irrelevant to French law.[17] He drew upon the work of historians, including Niebuhr, Thierry, Lerminier, and even Vico (via Michelet), but his professional judgments were based on exegesis of authoritative texts. As with the medieval scholastic tradition, Troplong did not allow historical fact to imply errors in the law. In discussing Roman law, for example, Savigny argued that possession was both fact and law; but in the context of modern French law, Troplong would admit no such unprofessional hybrid. Troplong seems indeed to fit the juridical pattern a recent critic has attributed to the conventions of the Code and its exegetes: the "rules of the bourgeois game, which was economic and, by implication, *sauve qui peut*." Did this represent the perfection or the bankruptcy of modern French jurisprudence?

As far as jurisprudence was concerned, however, the real controversy in these years before the revolutions of 1848 had to do with something more fundamental than methodology. Ultimately, it was over the viability of the claims of law to be the essential science of society. This claim had been made successfully for centuries, and it continued to be imposed upon each new class of law students. Jurisprudence was a "science" because it dealt with evidence in terms of cause and effect, and yet it was also the social "art of the good and the just"— so the civilians had taught, and so also their disciples, the commentators on the Civil Code. These claims were also quite in keeping with the "bourgeois monarchy" and its supporters, as they had been with previous regimes. To social and "socialist" critics, however, the failures of the legal system were becoming more and more apparent as the ideals of liberty and especially equality diverged from the realities of a society that, despite invocations like Michelet's of national unity, was obviously torn by class dissension. In retrospect, at least, Louis Blanc's analysis of contemporary history seems more appropriate than Michelet's vision.[18] The answer to Blanc's question "What is the bourgeoisie?" made it clear that the "people" were no longer, historically or legally, one. They were divided by that central principle of the Code, the primary rule of the "bourgeois game," "absolute private property."[19] In this sense, the decade before the revolutions of the mid-nineteenth century saw a pronounced divergence between history and law. Social radicalism in particular signaled an end to the alliance between Clio and Themis.

Many jurists and historians of course rejected this view and continued to expound their ideals from their professional positions. To the dismay of his students and former colleagues, Lerminier, for example, was led by his legalism, and his Germanism, to become in effect a bourgeois ideologist. Despite his flirtation with Saint-Simonianism, Lerminier, like the "grand commentators," was satisfied that modern French jurisprudence had reconciled the historical and philosophical schools through the Napoleonic codification. "A code," he observed, "is both a history and a system," and he tended to assume that it represented the best way to resolve mounting social questions.[20] So did his colleague and collaborator Ledru-Rollin, though 1848 would change his views. Another jurist who clung to legalism while professing revolutionary ideals was C. G. Hello, whose reflections on the "philosophy of history" and the need for a "social revolution" (through the legal profession) were cited earlier.[21] Like Lerminier he continued to believe that "social science" (both used this term) was the product of generations of effort by the giants of the legal tradition: Dumoulin, D'Aguesseau, Portalis, and the others.

But at that very moment, history was calling into question

these traditions and assumptions, and beneficiaries of legal traditionalism and the "German impulse" were swimming against the currents of social thought. By that same time P. J Proudhon ("the left Proudhon," to distinguish him from his distant cousin, the distinguished jurist, also from Besançon) had come to regard jurisprudence not as the gateway but as the primary obstacle to social reform. In 1844 Proudhon indeed thought about seeking a law degree, even of writing his thesis on "what is good in one of the Codes," but he found contemporary legal interpretation, especially that of the historical school, to be pernicious. To Proudhon the implication of historicism was the grounding of ideals in custom, a violation of the very idea of law. "It is a rule of jurisprudence," he wrote, "that the fact does not substantiate the right," whence the grounds for his notorious aphorism that "property is theft," or even "homicide."[22] Jurists talk on and on about the law, he lamented, but to the question "What is justice?" they have no answer. Old Regime jurists like Pothier assumed that social order was based on divine law and universal brotherhood, but as any fool could see, the fact was that brother fought brother in a competition regulated only by custom and convention—and by lawyers. Nor had this been changed by the Civil Code and its commentators. According to Toullier, Troplong, Laboulaye, and their colleagues, charged Proudhon, the civil state was "first despotism, then monarchy, then aristocracy, today democracy, but always tyranny."

Proudhon did not withhold praise from some scholars, such as Grimm and Michelet, for their insights into social history; but for modern jurisprudence he had only contempt. Not only was their so-called science based on hypocrisy, but their grasp of reality was almost negligible. "How could these men," he asked, "who never had the faintest idea of statistics, valuation, or political economy, furnish us with principles of legislation?"[23] There was a basis for justice neither in the "practical and conventional" (positivist and perhaps "Austinian") school nor in "the fatalistic and pantheistic school, sometimes called the historical school, which . . . maintains that law, like lit-

121

erature and religion, is always the expression of society." "These are respectively a *thesis* and *antithesis*," he concluded. "There remains to be found, then, a *synthesis*." And this synthesis would be a new rationalism, a modern philosophical school.

The most striking example of the backlash to the historical school and conventional jurisprudence is the case of the very young Marx. Before Proudhon moved to Paris and began to reflect on the law of property, Marx had already begun his formal legal studies. Indeed he was thrown into the very cockpit of juridical controversy: the *Methodenstreit* between Savigny and Gans, two of his teachers at the University of Berlin's law faculty in the late 1830s. The quarrel became public in 1839, when Gans issued his critique of Savigny's interpretation of the Roman law of possession, on grounds very similar to those not only of orthodox French jurists but also of Proudhon. It was absurd to assume that the ancient Romans had possessed philosophic truth, Gans argued, and still more so to hold with Savigny that "possession is a fact, a natural condition, and no right, but nevertheless the possessor as such has a right."[24] So an aspect of the Social Question replaced the problem of codification as the basic issue dividing the historical and philosophical schools.

At first, Marx inclined toward Gans and the "idealists," though he was also attracted to the "positive"—that is, empirical and scholarly—tendency of the "realist" party. He became deeply immersed in the legal tradition, including Heineccius and Old Regime scholarship as well as the Prussian and French code and modern jurisprudence. He began a translation of Justinian's *Digest* and even composed the major part of a treatise on modern law, a *Pandektensystem*, or sort of late scholastic contribution to the genre of what Savigny called legal "systematics." He followed the conventional "trichotomizing approach" (analogous to but independent of that of Hegel) and carried his analysis through the private law triad of persons, things, and actions. At the transition between private and public law, however, he "saw the falsity of the whole thing" and broke it off. He broke off his legal career, too, and in general his reasons illustrated with remarkable clarity the dilemma of jurisprudence and its relation with history in the second quarter of the nineteenth century.

The fallacy that Marx saw was what he called "the metaphysics of law." It stemmed from "the hopelessly incorrect division of the subject matter" and especially "the opposition between what is and what ought to be." More precisely, Marx concluded that the rules of private law were wholly conventional, that is, arbitrary, and did not receive their legitimation in the political ideals that subsumed them and purportedly established goals of justice and social welfare. What old-fashioned jurisprudence represented to Marx was a dogmatic formulation of the useful conventions of a status quo, or rather the doctrine of the rulers and beneficiaries of a status quo, and its professional champions. Even more than a private philosophy like Hegel's, a public code like Napoleon's embodied the expression not of "society" but of a ruling class and its legal defenders. In a word not yet used by Marx but already coined with the same pejorative connotations, law was an expression of "ideology." This was Marx's first recorded epiphany. "A curtain has fallen," he wrote to his father in 1837, "my holy of holies was rent asunder, and new gods had to be installed."

"Shortly after that," he wrote, "I pursued only positive studies," that is, historical and legal scholarship, especially the internal history of law, or as he preferred to put it, "positive law in its conceptual development." Like Proudhon, however, Marx rejected the notion of jurisprudence as a mere passive accumulation of this "positive law" as either the "expression of society" or legislative command. He directed his first polemical publications against these pernicious views, first in specific analyses of the evils of Prussian criminal law and censorship and in 1842 in a more theoretical attack on the historical school, whose leader (and Marx's former mentor) Savigny was then, of all things, Minister of Justice for the reform of the Prussian Code. In his "Philosophical Manifesto of the Historical School of Law," Marx not only announced

his abjuration of his first calling, the profession of law, but
also suggested some of the premises of a more critical and yet
more just science of society.[25] If only to avoid censorship,
Marx made his target not Savigny but his late colleague Hugo,
"forefather and prototype" (*Altvater* and *Naturmensch*) of the
historical school. What Marx objected to above all was the
mindless empiricism and professional complacency of Hugo.
"Everything serves him as an authority, every authority serves
him as an argument." Reinforcing this cynicism was the im-
moral motto of the historical school that was, in Marx's words,
that "the sole distinguishing feature of man is his animal nature." The conclusion, drawn also by Proudhon and other
critics, seemed to be that justice evolved naturally out of custom, hence that might produces right. Long after Marx had
abandoned jurisprudence, he was still fuming about this "school
which legitimates the baseness of today by the baseness of
yesterday . . . , a school to which history shows only its pos-
terior . . ." (referring to the mindless empiricism—the a pos-
teriori assumption—of the *Historische Rechtsschule*). This was
not an alliance between Themis and Clio; it was the enslave-
ment of the first by the second. And like Proudhon, Marx
appealed to philosophy and reason for an antidote.

Where could one look, then, for a way to a modern science
of society? Aside from a variety of quasi-religious philosophical systems, the trend seemed to be toward that "hardest" of
human disciplines, political economy, scorned as it was by
Hugo and his colleagues for its naïveté and detachment from
social values. But if economics was amoral, it was at least
rational; and many intellectuals, not only liberals, had shifted
their doctrinal allegiance. Among the most notable of these
were the editors of the Swiss *Annales de législation et de jurisprudence*, the historian Sismondi, and the young jurist Paolo
Rossi, who in fact was appointed by Guizot to teach political
economy at the Collège de France during the 1830s. From
one of Savigny's most devoted disciples, Rossi became an
equally enthusiastic salesman for the new "science" of economics. Just as in the 1820s he had proposed to transform

society on the basis of the new jurisprudence, so a decade later he saw social salvation through a larger and more realistic *haute science sociale* founded on political economy.[26] He continued to praise the old legal tradition—"Honneur aux auteurs du Code Civil!" he told his Parisian students—but he looked to economics for leadership during the next, industrial stage of society. From a very different political position and with a much less favorable opinion of the legal tradition, the younger Proudhon had come to the same conclusion.

But it was Marx who made the transition from the old art of law to the new science of economics most rigorously and rationally, and perhaps with a better appreciation of history. Having disposed of the historical school in 1842, Marx turned to a larger critique of Hegel. It was in this context that he began to emphasize as the exact opposite of the "speculative philosophy of law" what he called "praxis." The first item on his new agenda was not well-intentioned jurisprudence, but rather the crucial modern problem, which was "the relationship between industry and the political world."[27] With this on his mind Marx moved to Paris, "the new capital of the world," in the fall of 1843; and in that land of rationality (so he, like Heine, regarded it) "Charles" Marx finally installed his "new gods." Or rather, out of his reading of the classical economists (in which he was encouraged by Engels) he proposed to create the "true philosophy" that jurisprudence had claimed but always failed to be. Toward this ultimate social science Marx worked continuously, both through "ruthless criticism of everything existing," including polemics against such like-minded deviants as Proudhon, and, perhaps more importantly, through massive "positive" (which is to say the vicarious "praxis" of historical) studies. This was at least an indirect result of the early nineteenth-century convergence between Clio and Themis.

The works of Marx, Proudhon, and other subverters of normal jurisprudence and of the great jurists and many of the historians of the period converged on one problem. Representing at once the major accomplishment of the great Revo-

125

lution, the dominant theme of postrevolutionary jurisprudence, and the root of the looming and soon overwhelming Social Question, this problem was Proudhon's notorious query of 1840, "What is property?" To inquire into the nature of any institution in this period was to inquire also into its origins, and the genesis of private property indeed became an issue central to modern social thought. There has never been a satisfactory answer to this, still less to the Social Question, but the investigations into the background have been seminal for the development of modern historical and legal scholarship. In a sense, the study of the history of private property represents the strongest tie between history and law, and its published results, the most valuable product of that union.

The Question of Property

L'histoire du droit de propriété est un des plus
grands objets d'étude qui peussent être offerts
à la philosophie et à l'érudition.
—Giraud (1838)

L'esprit des lois, c'est la propriété.
—Marx (citing Linguet)

"Good God!" cried the younger Proudhon. "Whoever in-
quired into the origins of the rights of liberty, security, or
equality?"[1] His liberal nemesis Adolphe Thiers, in an attack
on the very work in which this question appeared, shared his
adversary's puzzlement. "How has it happened," Thiers asked
in 1848, "that property, the natural instinct of man, child,
and animal, single aim and indispensable reward of labor, has
been put in question?"[2] In France the question seemed especially offensive, even blasphemous. "Do we wish to know the
fixed idea, the ruling passion of the French peasant?" asked
Michelet. Just follow him on his Sunday walk as he goes to
see his mistress. "What mistress?" Michelet continued. "His
bit of land."[3] This passion was even more intense, if more
broadly conceived, with the bourgeoisie, who rose to power
through the religion of property, and most of all with their
devoted spokesmen, the lawyers and interpreters of the Code.

Why, then, put property to the question? There were many
reasons, as both Proudhon and Thiers knew; but besides the
overriding Social Question the main one was that for most
early nineteenth-century intellectuals, right and left, the
emergence of property represented the beginning of human
consciousness and so of history itself. In general, this was a
modern extension of John Locke's almost existentialist defini-

127

tion of property as man's "Life, Liberty, and Estate" and perhaps of Hegel's conception of it as the result of the imposition
of subjective "will" on the objective world of nature. Although represented by Locke as a "natural right" and by Hegel as a natural process, property also had, at least potentially,
a historical dimension, since it could be expanded indefinitely
in time by means of appropriation and especially human labor.[4] The success story of this notion, a cornerstone of the
theory of material progress as well as of modern political
economy, is too well known to need rehearsing here.

But if the proprietary theory of human nature—man as *homo
economicus* or *acquisitivus*—was a fairly recent discovery of philosophers, it had long been an assumption among civil lawyers. It had, indeed, been built into the very structure of law
almost from the beginning. Since at least the time of Gaius
(second century A.D.), civil law had possessed an all-encom-
passing, threefold schematization; namely, persons, things, and
actions.[5] Looking at law as an idealized expression of the field
of social action, one inferred that "action" signified the bridge
between "personality" and "reality." But more concretely, the
temporal pattern was the appropriation by "persons" of "things"
necessary for subsistence (for *res*, the second category, meant
primarily potential possessions or property) and the preservation or protection of property through "actions" at law. The
old legal tradition represented a much richer, or at least technically more elaborate, heritage of thought and interpretation
of the idea of property. Certainly it was closer to the thinking
of professional jurists. Nor did the jurists need Hegel (or Marx)
to show them the philosophical—and especially the historical—implications of the idea of property. "Since man has become aware of his individuality," wrote one nineteenth-century French lawyer, "he has become aware of external objects
and has sought to acquire them."[6] Potentially, this was a way
(in legal terms, the "private" rather than the "public" way) of
seeing and interpreting the whole course of western history;
even before Marx jurists were inclined professionally toward
this materialist conception, a conception that, moreover, was

in general accord with the premises of nineteenth-century historicism.

In the early nineteenth century the problem of private property represented a major intersection of practical and theoretical concerns, and it intensified the shift of the "new history" from an abstractly political to a concretely social focus. Fundamental to emergent "bourgeois" civilization, property was a central theme both of professional jurisprudence and of the historical school. On the practical side, Baron Locré pointed out that "men can be useful or destructive to one another with respect only to two things, one's person and one's property."[7] It is hardly an exaggeration to agree with him that "the subject of civil law is property," though it may be an exaggeration to add, with Troplong, that "the domain of property has been separated from every political element."[8] Another early commentator on the Code, Bousquet, put it more theoretically: "The law of property is the fundamental law on which all social institutions rest and is as precious as life itself, since it assures the means of preserving it."[9] Here indeed was the link with politics, for as Toullier wrote, "To property we owe the foundation of the civil state. Without the title of property it would never be possible to submit men to the salutary yoke of the law."[10]

The modern concept of private property was indissolubly linked with the great Revolution, to the extent indeed that some historians, Tocqueville and Taine among them, reversed the usual formula by making the Revolution the product instead of the source of modern property relations. In any case, the two together constituted the cornerstones of French unity. As a result of the night of 4 August 1789, the Jacobins became acquisitors, according to Michelet's aphorism, and the acquisitors, Jacobins. "Feudalism" was abolished, and the process of social transformation was carried further by legislative acts representing the national will. Superseding the unjust legalisms of the Old Regime was the idea of "absolute property," based on subsistence and the legitimizing force of labor (*travail* or *industrie*).[11] Formulated in terms taken from

129

Roman law, this conception was canonized in the Napoleonic Code. Implied by the Revolution, its Bonapartist extension, and the massive transfers of ownership was a coherent theory of the historical process; and the human will to acquisition and power was the key.

There were restrictions to this neat theory, however, and obstacles to this will. One difficulty arose from the perpetual conflict between the public and private spheres, specifically from confiscations (or "sacrifices," as jurists preferred to say) made in the name of "public utility."[12] Another and more complicated set of problems derived from the conflicting claims, especially after 1814, between "former" and "new proprietors" (*anciens* and *nouveaux propriétaires*), which often meant émigrés and more recent occupants either of so-called national lands (*biens dits nationaux*) or of those allegedly tainted with feudalism (*mélangé de féodalité*) or simply of undetermined ownership. In Restoration France it was unprecedentedly true that, as Toullier remarked, "the majority of disputes arising between men had to do with property."[13] Nor was "property" the only issue covering these social problems, for it overlapped with the two other aspects of what has been called the "classificatory genitive," that is, possession and prescription.[14] In any case, it was in this social context, and in the midst of massive publicity concerning property disputes and the political issue of indemnification for the émigrés, that property was "put in question." In particular, its origins were subjected to historical scrutiny, with history being regarded not only as the cause but also as the continuing basis of the legitimacy of social institutions.

There was a second and more theoretical context, and this was provided again by the historical school, specifically by Savigny's vastly influential treatise of 1803 on the Roman law of possession, which went through eight editions and generated an immense amount of scholarly controversy, of which repercussions are still heard.[15] Although some French jurists regarded the work as antiquarian and irrelevant to the concerns, it was in fact cited in works of jurisprudence and social

130

criticism. More to the point, it served to highlight the question of the origins of property and other aspects of the classificatory genitive. Of course, Roman law was juridically significant for modern French as well as German law, and Savigny's interpretations of the early parts of the tradition were weightily supplemented by the investigations of his friend Niebuhr into Roman agrarian history. In the first half of the nineteenth century, classical antiquity continued to furnish the primary model of social thought as well as of historical interpretation, and the scholarly work of these two giants of historiography was appealed to by social theorists and propagandists, right and left. Both figured centrally in the contemporary debates over the question so conventionally posed by the younger Proudhon (though so unconventionally and so brutally answered): "What is property?"

For the redactors property was the alpha and omega of civilization. "It is property that has established societies . . . ," declared Portalis, "that has vivified, extended, and enlarged our existence."[16] In general, property began with the principle of first occupancy and was justified by labor. To this social process the law gave theoretical form and protection, and it was the task of professional and academic jurists to apply it to particular cases and to elaborate its implications, philosophical as well as legal and social. Property represented in the first place self-consciousness, since it was based on the essential distinction between mine and thine (*meum et tuum; le mien et le tien*) and implied the intention to keep. By extension, it could also be identified (as Cousin, Thiers, and others identified it) with individuality, liberty, and history itself. It began with individual consciousness, for as Troplong wrote, "Property is human liberty exercised over physical nature. . . . As soon as there were men, there were proprietors."[17]

How did it all begin? In order to answer this question it was necessary, wrote J.-M. Carou, an authority on possession, "to go back in thought to the times when [civilized] men appeared on earth."[18] It was a time, many thought, when there was no need to distinguish between property and possession,

131

and of course no need for prescription. Perhaps there was no need for lawyers (one of the visions of Old Regime society, too). But thereafter, it seemed to jurists, the legal development of property was congruent with the trajectory of history itself. According to the most common view, expressed classically and yet "for the most part historically" by Louis Dunod in 1730, "ownership [*domain*] began with occupation, which is a kind of possession," and "therefore possession should be regarded as the principle and foundation of prescription."[19] Whence the simple sequence of possession, prescription, property. This concatenation was also assumed by many postrevolutionary jurists, such as the elder Proudhon, for whom possession was the "cause" of property. "Possession is the fact, property the law," jurists liked to repeat, and the history of society was by inference the transition from one to the other.[20]

Conveniently and convergently, this legal interpretation suited the historical pattern established by Turgot and Adam Smith of four evolutionary stages of growth: hunting, pasturage, agriculture, and commerce. In his pioneering commentary on modern French law (1803), the old *philosophe* Bernardi divided the "origins of real property" into three stages, from savagery (*peuples sauvages*) to pasturage (*pasteurs*) to agriculture (*agricoles*), pointing out the vestiges of these primitive conditions in the provincial customs of France.[21] The legal counterpart of this trajectory began, as Toullier taught, with the natural "right of first occupancy," becoming permanent with "agriculture" and evolving into "full property."[22] According to Carou, the stages of the civilizing processes included a "savage" stage of first occupancy, then one of natural and civil possession, and finally the period of property and proprietary society.[23] Such was the legal version of the theory of "progress," which would grow and flourish in the nineteenth century, finding authoritative expression in the work of Thiers and his juridical counterpart Troplong, and becoming virtually the official ideology of the July Monarchy, as well as a basis for interpreting the long-term pattern of history.

Technically, this view was contradicted by Savigny, for

whom possession was "both fact and law" and, according to the famous civilian formula, "had nothing in common with property" (*nihil commune habet proprietas cum possessione*), historically or legally.[24] The investigations of Niebuhr seemed to reinforce this interpretation, since the original public land of the Roman republic (*ager publicus* or *Romanus*) was open only to possession and was distinct from property (*dominium*), which pertained strictly to family ownership. For Niebuhr, who did not hesitate to express his disgust at the "frantic levelers" of the late revolution in France, this was also a satisfying revelation, showing as it did that property was indeed "private" from the beginning. In general, he gave scholarly endorsement to the juridical alliance between law and property. "All legislators and especially Moses," Niebuhr wrote, "have based the success of their institutions, justice, and good citizenship on landed property, or at least on hereditary possession in favor of the greatest possible number of citizens."[25]

The distinction between property and possession troubled French jurists on philosophical as well as historical grounds, and yet it could not be denied. "There is a war," wrote Carou, "On the one side [there is] the abstract right of property, on the other the fact of possession," and, quoting Troplong, "on the one hand an inert and fragile principle, on the other an activity profitable to the state; decadence on the one hand, progress on the other."[26] To resolve this dilemma some jurists denied the relevance of Savigny's arguments; his work, complained W. Belime, reads as if composed by a second-century jurist (he must have meant Gaius).[27] The "sacred" and therefore original character of property must be defended at all costs. "I shall go further," wrote Belime. "Not only was the sentiment of property born with the world, but it was first-born, and the idea of possession came only afterward." "God forbid," wrote another jurist of the July Monarchy, "that I should think or write that property was a purely arbitrary institution! I do not hesitate to proclaim that its source is divine, its origin eternal."[28]

The same view toward the "sacred character" of property

was taken by jurists who were willing to acknowledge that it had indeed originated in contingent possession. This interpretation was in keeping both with the general principle that law began in fact (*lex ex facto oritur*) and with another Roman formula (contradicting Savigny's) that "property commenced with possession." It was in keeping, too, with the revolutionary basis of modern French jurisprudence.[29] Troplong was the great spokesman for this position, and he rested his defense both on the principle of labor (property was the *fille du travail*) and on the factor of time. A right could not be established by lapse of time alone (and here Troplong cited Vico approvingly), for human intention was also needed, and yet history did seem to be on the side of the proprietors. "Consecrated by time," Troplong wrote, "property will be thereby regarded as legitimate and authentic through a sort of mystical fiction that encourages the public interest."[30] What economists took to be the Invisible Hand, jurists tended to see as the Hand of God. It was in this general context that Troplong presented his juridical paean to "progress," though he by no means accepted the arguments of the economists that continual productivity was needed to justify property. On the contrary, he wrote, "Once acquired by occupation and labor, it is naturally conserved not only by these means but also by the intention not to surrender it."[31] Such were the "rules of the bourgeois game," if not the laws of history.

Practical jurisprudence had to face the historical question of property. Despite the simplified definition offered by the Code, the level of disagreement was remarkable, especially since defenders of the émigrés, jurists such as Bergasse and Dard, argued for the restoration of their clients' land on precisely these grounds.[32] Confiscation of noble lands was illegal and "against nature" from the beginning, according to some publicists who tried at the very least to supply moral arguments for the principle of indemnification, recognized indeed in the Code. There were other problems of legal, and so historical, continuity. Prescription normally "did not run" over the caesura created by the great Revolution. Yet in fact like

Old Regime jurisprudence in general, many specific claims, at least those not flagrantly tainted with feudalism, carried over into Restoration times, explicitly as well as (through the devices of possession and prescription) implicitly. Even more controversial was the issue of confiscation on grounds of "public utility." Along with the problem of possession, this served to provoke the most famous formulation of Proudhon's "What is property?"[33] All of these problems were tied in with the history and origins of private property.

The "religion of property" reflected in these opinions had an impact on historical scholarship as well as on jurisprudence. In his book on the history of Roman property dedicated to Thiers, Charles Giraud celebrated his subject in 1838 as "one of the greatest that could be offered to philosophy and to erudition."[34] "Property is man," he declared, "but only civilized man." Further, "On the law of property depend the culture of the inhabitable world, the guarantee and morality of labor, the application of justice, all morality, and all public order." So it had been with the Romans, and Giraud also referred to the Roman public land in this connection, though (in opposition to Niebuhr and in support of Montesquieu) he believed that such land was open not just to patricians but to all citizens. In any case, he repeated (as Marx would a few years later) Niebuhr's telling anecdote about the Roman king Numa, who established territorial boundaries, marked by representations of the god Terminus, even before religious rites. In his book published the next year, Laboulaye added that crimes against property constituted sacrilege against *ce dieu Terme*. This work extended the field of inquiry to western history as a whole and with heavier reliance on the historical school, though on the essential point of the origins of property he seemed to depart from his mentor in his conclusion that "the fact became a law; this law is property." But it was surely in the spirit of the historical school that Laboulaye attempted to frame the question in strictly historical and "realistic" terms— not the lawyers' problem, "What is property?" but the human dilemma, "To whom belongs the soil?"[35]

The dilemma caused by the relationship between property and possession provided the context for another issue that had historical as well as moral implications: the old idea of primitive communism. To the redactors of the Code, of course, this was anathema. Portalis, for example, had expressed his contempt for speculations about originally communal land (*biens originairement communs*), and commentators on the Code routinely followed him in this prejudice.[36] So did orthodox academicians like Laboulaye and Charles Giraud, for whom the notion was a retrospective utopianism hardly less imaginary than the fictions of More, Campanella, and Rousseau.[37] Yet the Roman model was ambiguous, for alongside the paternal and proprietary pattern was the communal land, the *ager publicus*, which seemed to furnish a precedent for "another mode of possession," in the words of Paolo Grossi.[38] The notion of "original communism" was also supported by orthodox jurists, as Proudhon pointed out, among them Grotius and other devotees of natural law.[39] This tradition Proudhon much preferred to the "fabulous and perhaps scandalous history" propagated by such pedants as his cousin, the elder Proudhon, and supported by the hypocrisies of what he scorned as "bourgeois morality."

For Proudhon and like-minded critics, among them the young Marx, the main trouble was in the modern confusion between property and possession, and especially in the notion that the first issued historically from the second. This was exactly the objection registered by Marx (and before him Hegel) against Hugo, Savigny, and the historical school, that it based legal principle on contingent custom, right on might. But Proudhon's target was really the legal profession as a whole. "We are very far," he wrote, "from the eclogues of MM. Troplong, Thiers, Cousin, Sudre, and Laboulaye on property and its legitimation by labor, first occupancy, affirmation of self, and other sentimental considerations."[40] Behind these fictions lay the historical truth of the matter, which was that "individual *possession* is the condition of social life." Toward the end of his life, Proudhon still found it necessary to "warn the reader to take care to distinguish possession, which everybody, learned and ignorant alike and even legists, confuse with property, giving the name of the one to the other."

Long before the appearance of Proudhon's inflammatory pamphlet, the issue of primitive communism had invaded the field of historical scholarship, and once again this was due in part to the German impulse. The Romantic vision of a free peasant community (the *Markgenossenschaft*) can be traced back to Justus Möser's *History of Osnabrück*, which began to appear in 1768; but insistence on its communistic character was really the work of writers from the historical school, especially Eichhorn and Jakob Grimm. In France this "Germanist" thesis was taken over primarily by Michelet, whose *Origins of French Law* of 1838 combined distillations of Roman and Germanic experience in a Vichian solvent.[41] In his "second memoir" of 1841, Proudhon was happy to call both Michelet and Grimm as witnesses to his defense.[42] Yet Michelet also celebrated the development of private property, suggesting in his "poetical" fashion that the prehistorical rite of occupation was a sort of marriage and later, in *The People* of 1846, that this relationship was one of the roots of national unity and strength. In general, private property was "the ruling passion of the French peasant," wrote Michelet, and France would be the last of the great nations to renounce this institution.[43] Such was the point of departure of his famous enterprise celebrated in that work as historical "resurrection."

After mid-century the idea of primitive communism became increasingly popular among scholars, especially in response to Georg von Maurer's investigations into the village community, which were taken up enthusiastically by Marx and Engels and developed independently by such founders of ethnographical theory as McLennan and Lewis Henry Morgan.[44] The *Communist Manifesto* of 1847 lamented the class divisions created by the institution of private property; but in a later edition, Engels (who himself wrote an essay on the *Mark*) amended this declaration to read, "The *written* history of all hitherto existing society is the history of class struggles," in

137

the light of the work of Maurer, Morgan, and others, who revealed "the inner organization of this primitive Communistic society." To others this view remained a backward-looking utopianism, a reversion to the dreams of More or Campanella. As Giraud had rejected such interpretations of Roman history as fiction (*roman*), so his successor of the next generation, Fustel de Coulanges, denounced the Romantic Germanism of Maurer and, in France, of Paul Viollet in favor of the orthodox conception of private property (and with it, presumably, the bourgeois family) as primordial and immemorial—and equally mythical.[45] The fundamental ideological conflict within jurisprudence was thus carried over into modern historical scholarship, another somewhat belated result of the encounter between Clio and Themis.

CHAPTER TWELVE

The End of the "New History"

> L'histoire des peuples est une échelle de misère
> dont les révolutions forment les différents
> degrés.
>
> —Chateaubriand (1797)

Montesquieu's dictum that "history illuminates law, and laws history" was never so well illustrated as in the generation before the revolutions of 1848.[1] The encounters between Clio and Themis were on the whole mutually reinforcing, with the muse of history turning to the goddess of justice for materials, methods, and values, and providing in return a sense of social reality, process, and perspective. The alliance was strengthened by intellectual reactions to the great Revolution, then by attempts to continue it by evolutionary means and identification with the idea of progress. In a sense, history and law joined in the support of the revolution of 1830 and in establishing the ideological basis of the July Monarchy. For historians like Guizot and Michelet, 1830 marked the culmination of national history; for lawyers like Dupin and Troplong, it marked also the apogee of their profession; and the future appeared bright for both—an "eternal July," in Michelet's words.

Such was the intellectual background of the "new history" proclaimed by Thierry and others, the great enterprise of restoring the national past in all of its color and institutional complexity. Out of the conjunction between history and law came one of the most remarkable and productive episodes in the history of historical scholarship. Like the Romantic literary movement with which it was affiliated, the new history was concerned not only with the popular and emotional dimensions of the past but also with the deepest possible per-

139

spective, that is, with prehistorical origins. The peculiar Romantic sense of time was shared by historians and jurists. The characteristic effort to think one's way back through time (*remonter* was the key word) has been pointed out with respect to poets, including Lamartine and Vigny, but it invaded less elegant branches of literature as well.[2] Citing the words of Portalis, Laferrière, for example, proposed that "in order to understand French law, it was necessary to go back to Roman law" (*remonter au droit romain*). In his study of possessory law, Carou asked his readers to go back in thought (*remonter par la pensée*) to primitive times. Indeed much of the historical investigation of private property involved efforts to divine the human condition in prehistorical terms—not to explain it in terms of cause and effect but to evoke and give meaning to it synthetically if not poetically.[3]

One of the primary conditions for the "new history" was the increasing prestige of "positive" research and knowledge, as derived from the social as well as the natural world. Though developed most systematically by the "prophets of Paris" and appropriated nominally by Auguste Comte, "positivism" in a more general sense was characteristic of many aspects of nineteenth-century "science," which leaned self-consciously from a rational to an empirical mode of investigation.[4] This impulse was apparent in a number of fields, including jurisprudence, which relied on a massive accumulation of cases, decisions, and precedents, and in the study of history, which entered a heroic age of archival research and documentation. Resistance to the philosophical school in general and Hegelianism in particular was evident in both areas. The old sage Goethe, for example, advised the Hegelian Gans of the desirability of attending to the concrete and, as he put it, "also coming into contact with the empiricists,"[5] while much of Ranke's career was devoted to the rejection of idealist historiography. Fascination with "positive" knowledge was evident, too, in the increased interest in statistical and demographical information as a basis for social science and policy. The years 1830 to 1850 have been called the "age of enthusiasm" in the history of statistics,[6] and only from this period are such data sufficiently reliable for historians. The concern for the construction of a hard and quantitative science of society is reflected in the writing of liberals and socializing radicals alike.

Also important for historical studies were the rise and intellectual hegemony achieved by the "social," understood in largely pejorative contrast to the political (as, by analogy, jurisprudence was contrasted to legislation). The revolutionary experience, according to the interpretation of Lorenz von Stein, produced first the concept of "society" itself and the "social movement," then the "Social Question," and finally, social revolution.[7] The legal, institutional, and social historiography of the second quarter of the century interacted with this process, to the extent at least that it looked beyond the drums and the trumpets, kings and courts, to the role of the Third Estate, urban society, and especially the development of private property. In this shift of interest the erudition and methods of the German historical school was crucial. In the long run, however, French scholars brought and kept their interpretations into line with French ideological issues, above all those issues associated with the revolution of 1830, even when they seemed to have only an antiquarian value. In a period in which the nature of property was equated with its origins, a work like Giraud's study of Roman property or Pardessus' edition of the Salian Law (touching as it did on the issue of primitive communism) could be relevant and even controversial.

But the new history, like the new jurisprudence of the Code, was the product of a time of stability, or at least of optimism and a certain complacency. History and law were both placed in the service of middle-class "progress" in order to explain, legitimize, and in various ways celebrate the heritage and brilliant future of national civilization. As illustrated by the respective views taken toward private property, the central bourgeois institution, neither field seemed prepared or equipped to confront the social questions provoked by the inequalities of property in a commercial and industrializing society. Like literature, historiography is (to paraphrase Bonald's famous aphorism) "the expression of society"; and the historiography of the July Monarchy, along with its jurisprudence, displayed many of the qualities, especially the complacency, the optimism, and the egoism, of the "conquering bourgeoisie." Despite endless discussion of "revolution," neither historians nor jurists were ready to comprehend the drift of events in the 1840s, when the Social Question was transformed into the Political Question.

The February revolution "surprised" practically everyone, right and left, from Guizot to Marx. For Guizot, of course, the clock had stopped in July 1830, as it had for many historians and jurists for whom social change had become identified with bourgeois progress. As Guizot's career showed, historical understanding could do nothing to salvage the July Monarchy, nor even to make sense of the "social revolution" that overtook it, while the old jurisprudence was largely bankrupt, along with the political establishment it served. Like the pre-1789 Order of Advocates, the legal profession had become compromised, if not corrupted, to the extent suggested by Daumier's caricatures, as well as distracted from its claims either to science or to justice. In conceptual terms, the "positive" had to be more focused and systematic than professional jurisprudence or the "new history"; and the "social," tainted increasingly by pejorative notions of class division, seemed even less amenable to old-fashioned scholarship, which seemed irreconcilable with a viable "social science."

One aspect of this change of intellectual climate was the fact that the center of attention shifted increasingly from property to labor. "Everything comes from labor," Proudhon declared. Yet labor was a problem that had to be grasped and grappled with, not through the old legal tradition or academic historicism but rather through "scientific" analysis—and perhaps direct, extra-legal action, whether administrative or revolutionary. The view that liberals took toward the accumulation of wealth, Proudhon took toward social justice, that is, that it had to be derived not from history but from nature, not deduced from the Code, but "calculated."[8] The same inclination can be seen in the thought of the young Marx, whose "critique of Hegelian philosophy of law" led not only from theory to "praxis" but also from idealist complaints about social evils to modern "politico-reality," starting with the structure of capitalism and ensuing class division.[9]

In a word, as Proudhon wrote in 1847, "The revolution today is political economy," and what Louis Dumont has called "the triumph of economic ideology" was indeed a more permanent result than any of the temporary gains of the February revolution.[10] In France the campaign for this was carried on above all by the *Journal des économistes*, which was in a sense political economy's answer to *La Thémis* and its successors. During the 1840s this journal featured articles on legal and historical as well as economic topics, though its main focus was such subjects as demography, commercial and industrial conditions, and the contemporary financial crisis. Other articles urged the study of political economy, regularly reported on the course given by Michel Chevalier (who succeeded Rossi in the chair in the Collège de France) and in the spring of 1848 protested the temporary suppression of the teaching of this subject.[11] More significantly, perhaps, the *Journal des économistes* addressed itself not only to the expansion of and threats to wealth and production but also to poverty, crime, *la misère* and other aspects of the Social Question. Concerned more with the facts of inequality than with the theory of equality and hopes of solidarity, this periodical and its readers were better prepared to cope with the upheavals of '48 than were observers tied to the conventions of jurisprudence.

One of the byproducts of the ascendancy of political economy in this period was the rise of interest in economic history, at first mainly as a chronicle of economic success but increasingly in the context of broader social concerns, for instance in the work of Auguste Blanqui, founder of the *Journal des économistes*.[12] Most crucial, as usual, was the contribution of Germany, beginning especially with the work of Wilhelm Röscher, founder of the so-called first historical school of economics.[13] In general, economic history had lagged behind other branches of the discipline because, unlike other institutions of the French monarchy, it lacked archival traditions or collections like that assembled by Thierry for the Third Estate. But social turmoil turned scholarly attention to lower levels of society, and in 1858 Guizot's Académie des Sciences Morales et Politiques offered a prize for a historical work on the working classes. The result was the pioneering book by Emile Levasseur, the first classic of French economic history.[14]

Like jurisprudence in more settled times, political economy was anxious to establish ties with neighboring fields, especially with the law, though presumably from a position of advantage. Links with jurisprudence were strengthened when the chair of political economy, first provided for in 1819, was finally granted to the law faculty of Paris in 1863. Its first tenant, Anselme Batbie, insisted on the connection, proclaiming to the beginning law students that "above all I am a jurisconsult" and citing the formula of Roman law, "We are priests, consecrated to the cult of justice."[15] Outside the law faculty the relationship was less cordial, and again the sticking point was the problem of labor. To Chevalier's successor Henri Baudrillart, for example, the jurists' "mystical" views of property were nonsense.[16] Property depended neither on legal convention nor on religion, but only on the economic reality of labor. "Travail!" he rhapsodized. "Quel mot j'ai prononcé!" In the "religion of property," indeed, labor had replaced divine sanction as final as well as first cause.

One important intellectual development of the later nineteenth century may be attributed at least indirectly to the alliance between history and law, and that is the infant discipline of anthropology, understood in a new and "scientific" sense.[17] Many of its founders were jurists and at least honorary members of the historical school, and the questions addressed had been posed by this same school, starting with the origins of private property and including problems of family and kinship. Social and cultural anthropology originated in investigations of primitive and comparative law, especially under the impulse of the historical school. Although limited

144

at first mainly to the Indo-European field and cultivated by Romantic linguistic and legal scholarship and imagination, the new science of anthropology soon expanded beyond these parochial and legalistic boundaries through the combined influence of evidence collected from extra-European societies and the theory of social evolution. Yet the set of problems examined by the historical school was preserved—the origins of society, the question of property, and the hypothesis of primitive communism—although the context of the discussion was enriched through consideration of the tribe, the family, and the ethnological counterpart of original collectivism, which was matriarchal or at least matralinear society. The work of such pioneers of ethnological theory as Maine, Bachofen, Morgan, and Lavelaye—all jurists—represents the last repercussions of the encounter between Clio and Themis.

For the most part, however, neither the new history nor the old jurisprudence, tied as they were to faith in social institutions and national unity, survived the upheavals of 1848. Michelet tried to keep the faith, but the period of euphoria (and intellectual experimentation) was past, and so on the whole was the fruitful partnership between Clio and Themis. The enthusiastic *chasse aux documents* continued,[18] but the large vision of historical "resurrection" was lost in the experience of a real social revolution. The historiography of the July Monarchy, like its jurisprudence, had become apologetic, bound in a sense to official values and so incapable of moving with times that had diverged from these values. What, in such times, was the institution of monarchy? What was democracy? What were society, religion, and philosophy? Proudhon's answers were extreme but in keeping with the dislocations of the 1840s. If property was theft and law a sham, royalty was a "myth," democracy "chaos," society a "war," religion a "dream," and philosophy "hallucination."[19] And what else could history be (though Proudhon does not pose this question explicitly) but self-delusion?

The upshot was that from mid-century law and history were faced once again with tasks of reconstruction, but this time

145

going in divergent ways. Both aspired to "scientific" status, whether pursued through "positive" or "philosophical," empirical or rational, means. Jurisprudence had the choice of retreating to "positivism" (no connection to Comtean philosophy) or trying to catch up with the times by applying to modern disciplines such as economics, sociology, or anthropology. Perhaps most fundamental was the movement toward a socialized jurisprudence (*droit social*, companion to *économie sociale*) that, like Marx, rejected legal metaphysics and tried to confront (if only to paper over) problems of industrial society and class division.[20] According to this school, property, for example, was neither an abstract right nor an arbitrary condition but rather a "social function" to be assessed in terms of "social utility" or "economic utility," without much concern for history.[21]

History on the other hand tended to disengage itself from social questions and to devote itself to value-free investigations, especially of the national past. Perhaps the most characteristic, or rather prophetic, statement was the essay published by the young Ernest Renan in 1848, *The Future of Science*. A protégé at that time of Thierry, Renan was an admirer and indeed a product of what he called "the revolution that since 1830 has completely changed the face of historical studies." Like the young Marx, Renan turned toward "positive science" but very much away from the modish Positive Philosophy of Comte, who seemed to him (as Hegel seemed to Marx) a throwback to scholasticism. Renan was also disillusioned as well as distracted by the fruitless upheavals of 1848. For him "science is independent of every social form"; its future would be guaranteed not by partisan apologetics but by "simple curiosity," not by ideology but by erudition, not by "logophilia" (his own coinage) but by "philology," which was "the science of the products of the human spirit."[22] History and not nature, then, was the main target of this new "critical philosophy." In this connection, Renan invoked older scholarly traditions, including those of Muratori, Mabillon and the Benedictines, Vico, and Herder, as well as the recent achievements of Guizot, Thierry, Michelet, and German scholarship beginning with Niebuhr, though not exclusively the historical school of law.

To this old humanistic enterprise, the contemporary profession of law and the Social Question seemed largely irrelevant. Renan, turning his attention away from the "dream" of "egalitarian civilization," addressed himself to problems that, though antiquarian, seemed to him more meaningful and eventually, perhaps, more useful. Above all was the "problem of the *origins of humanity*," which Renan divided into six categories: the ethnographic question (diffusion versus independent development of races, languages, and so on); the chronological question (times of appearance of particular societies); the geographic question (places of these appearances); the physiological question (biological bases of development); the psychological question (beginnings of language, thought, and literature); and finally, the historical question (culmination of the "science of the origins of humanity").[23] This hope of going back to "origins" was, like Renan's Chateaubriandesque concentration on the history of religion, a Romantic notion, but the methods would be those of an age of Realism and of Science.

So history, the great "task and aptitude" of the age, was becoming more prominent than ever in the second half of the nineteenth century, even though divorced from jurisprudence, indeed social science in general, and for the most part from the Social Question. Reinforced by another sort of "German impulse," history became value-free and "scientific." After 1870, it was increasingly professionalized, especially through the establishment of chairs of ancient and modern history and through periodicals such as the *Revue des questions historiques* (1866), *Revue historique* (1871), and even more specialized publications that replaced *La Thémis* and its successors, and the *Revue des deux mondes* and other general and "encyclopedic" refuges for historical articles.[24] Meanwhile, the other branches of human culture to which history had "fallen heir" (according to Sainte-Beuve) were in the process of establishing their own

147

sorts of "scientific" status. As a result and despite technical improvements, history was in a sense returned to older and narrower channels—similar to the fate of other "new histories," before and since. But we should not let the accomplishments of the "scientific history" of the age of Ranke obscure the pioneering work of the older, pre-1848, new history, to which Gabriel Monod in the first issue of the *Revue historique* referred as "the golden age of historical writing in France." This generation was the one that, especially through the alliance with law, posed most fundamentally (and began gathering materials for) what Sainte-Beuve called "that terrible question" humanity put to itself: "Where have I come from? Why do I exist? Where am I going?"[25] From our vantage point Restoration historians failed to find satisfactory answers. Yet the questions themselves, value-laden as they may be, are surely worth pursuing—and perhaps especially by historians.

NOTES

NOTES TO CHAPTER ONE

1. Herbert Butterfield, *Man on His Past* (Cambridge, 1955), and Lord Acton's inaugural lecture on "The Study of History," in *Lectures on Modern History* (New York, 1950), with copious notes on the theory and practice of history in nineteenth-century Europe.
2. Pitrim Sorokin, *Fads and Foibles in Modern Sociology* (Chicago, 1956), chap. 1.
3. See below, chap. 2, n. 16.
4. The reference is to Thomas Kuhn, *The Structure of Scientific Revolutions*, 2d ed. (Chicago, 1970), and the massive commentary it has produced.
5. See below, chap. 3, n. 28.
6. Augustin Thierry, *Lettres sur l'histoire de France*, 13th ed. (Paris, 1868), 3.
7. Refer to my *Foundations of Modern Historical Scholarship* (New York, 1970), and for more recent literature see my review articles in *Journal of Modern History* 47 (1975), 679–90, and 54 (1982), 320–26. See also below, chap. 2, n. 35.
8. See below, chap. 10, n. 12.
9. Keith Baker, "On the Problem of the Ideological Origins of the French Revolution," *Modern Intellectual History*, ed. D. La Capra and S. Kaplan (Ithaca, 1982), 197–219.
10. Kuhn, *The Structure of Scientific Revolutions*, 116.
11. Montesquieu, *De l'Esprit des lois*, book 31, chap. 2.
12. See below, chap. 6.
13. Hayden White, *Metahistory* (Baltimore, 1973), and Lionel Gossman's *Augustin Thierry and Liberal Historiography*, History and Theory, Beiheft 15 (1976).
14. See below, chap. 8.

NOTES TO CHAPTER TWO

1. C. A. Sainte-Beuve, article on Guizot in *Lundi*, 21 October 1861, cited by Irving Babbitt in *Modern Masters of French Criticism* (New York, 1912), 263.
2. Auguste Comte, *Politique positive*, vol. 3, 1, cited by Acton in

Lectures on Modern History (New York, 1950), 338, notes to his inaugural lecture on the study of history.

3. Jules Michelet, *The People*, trans. G. H. Smith (New York, 1846), 25; and see below, chap. 9.

4. Georges Gusdorf, *Les Sciences humaines et la pensée occidentale*, vol. 8, *La Conscience révolutionnaire* (Paris, 1978), 504ff.

5. René de Chateaubriand, *Etudes historiques* (Paris, 1831), preface.

6. Henri Bordier, *Les Archives de la France* (Paris, 1855), 2ff.

7. See below, chap. 5, n. 3.

8. René de Chateaubriand, *Génie du Christianisme*, vol. 1 (Paris, n.d.), 29.

9. Sainte-Beuve, *Portraits contemporains*, vol. 4 (Paris, 1889), 125–362. In general see G. P. Gooch, *History and Historians in the Nineteenth Century* (London, 1920), chap. 9; Eduard Fueter, *Geschichte der neueren Historiographie* (Berlin, 1936); and René Wellek, *A History of Modern Criticism*, vol. 3 (New Haven, 1965), chap. 1.

10. B. J. Dacier, *Rapport historique sur le progrès de l'histoire et de la littérature ancienne depuis 1789* (Paris, 1810), prepared for Napoleon, 20 February 1808, especially 168ff. Ten years later, M. J. Chenier, in *Tableau historique de l'état et des progrès de la littérature française depuis 1789* (Paris, 1818), had little to add. In general see June K. Burton, *Napoleon and Clio: Historical Writing, Teaching and Thinking during the First Empire* (Durham, N.C., 1979), which tells us, among other things, that in 1811 there were 118 works published in history in 166 volumes on 3,665,000 sheets of paper.

11. J. M. Degérando, *Histoire comparée des systèmes de philosophie relativement aux principes des connaissances humaines* (Paris, 1804), tracing five "époques philosophiques," ending with that of Bacon and Locke. Degérando also published a *Programme du cours de droit public positif et administratif* (Paris, 1819).

12. Lord Acton, *Historical Essays and Studies* (London, 1907), 307.

13. See below, chap. 6, n. 4.

14. Acton, *Lectures on Modern History*, 14.

15. Jean Sarazin, *Du Progrès des études historiques en France au dix-neuvième siècle* (Strasbourg, 1835), 17ff. in reference particularly to Thierry, Michelet, Sismondi, Barante, Chateaubriand, Guizot, Villemain, Thiers, and Mignet.

16. See D. R. Kelley, "History as a Calling: The Case of La Popelinière," in *Renaissance Studies in Honor of Hans Baron*, ed. A. Molho and J. Tedeschi (Florence, 1971), 773–89; cf. Carl Becker, *The Heavenly City of the Eighteenth-Century Philosophers* (New Haven,

1932), chap. 3, and James Harvey Robinson, *The New History* (New York, 1912).

17. The most valuable general studies are B. Reizov, *L'Historiographie romantique française 1815–1830* (Moscow, n.d.), Stanley Mellon, *The Political Uses of History* (Stanford, 1958), P. Moreau, *L'Histoire en France au XIXe siècle* (Paris, 1935), F. Engel-Janosi, *Four Studies in French Romantic Historical Writing* (Baltimore, 1955), and P. Stadter, *Geschichtschreibung und historischen Denken in Frankreich 1789–1871* (Zurich, 1948). See also Alfred Nettement, *Histoire de la littérature française sous le gouvernement de Juillet*, vol. 2 (Paris, 1876), 334ff., and Robert Flint, *History of the Philosophy of History* (New York, 1894).

18. Chateaubriand, *Etudes historiques*, preface.

19. E. Coornaert, *Destins de Clio en France depuis 1800* (Paris, 1977), 20.

20. See the general discussion in Douglas Johnson, *Guizot, Aspects of French History* (London, 1963), chap. 7, and C. Pouthas, *Guizot pendant la Restauration* (Paris, 1923).

21. Beyond the "portraits" of Sainte-Beuve and the works cited in n. 15, I shall not provide bibliographical guidance here except to note the recent study of Yvonne Knibiehler, *Mignet, Historien liberal 1796–1884* (Lille, 1970).

22. Prosper de Barante, *Histoire des ducs de Bourgogne*, 6th ed. (Paris, 1839), 10.

23. Augustin Thierry, *Lettres sur l'histoire de France*, 13th ed. (Paris, 1868), 3.

24. R. Smithson, *Augustin Thierry* (Geneva, 1972), 307; and see Lionel Gossman, *Augustin Thierry and Liberal Historiography*, History and Theory, Beiheft 15 (1976).

25. Augustin Thierry, *Dix ans d'études historiques*, 11th ed. (Paris, 1868).

26. Augustin Thierry, *Essai sur l'histoire de la formation et le progrès du Tiers Etat*, 4th ed. (Paris, 1866), 33; and cf. Thierry, *Dix ans*, 244ff.

27. See below, chap. 5, n. 29.

28. Cited in Maxime Leroy, *Histoire des idées sociales en France*, vol. 2 (Paris, 1950), 418.

29. See especially Ernst Cassirer, *The Problem of Knowledge: Science and History Since Hegel* (New Haven, 1950), and Maurice Mandelbaum, *History, Man and Reason* (Baltimore, 1971).

30. A useful survey of the older literature is provided by Lord Acton, *Lectures on the French Revolution* (London, 1910), 345ff.; see

also Paul Farmer, *France Reviews Its Revolutionary Origins* (New York, 1944) and, more recently, H. Helsing, *Die Deutung der französischen Revolution in der französischen Historiographie* (Cologne, 1971).

31. The classic work is still Friedrich Meinecke, *Die Entstehung des Historismus* (Berlin, 1936). Cf. Peter Hanns Reill, *The German Enlightenment and the Rise of Historicism* (Berkeley, 1975), and pushing the concept further back, Erich Hassinger, *Empirisch-rationaler Historismus* (Munich, 1978).

32. Pierre-Simon Ballanche, *Essais de palengénésis sociale*, vol. 2 (Paris, 1829); and see A. J. George, *Pierre-Simon Ballanche, Precursor of Romanticism* (Syracuse, 1945), 97.

33. Terry Clark, *Prophets and Patrons* (Cambridge, Mass., 1973), 22.

34. Louis de Bonald, *Législation primitive*, vol. 2 (Paris, 1817), 228. In general see Roger Picard, *Le Romantisme social* (New York, 1944), and Harry Levin, *The Gates of Horn* (Oxford, 1963).

35. The context and background of the present study is suggested in the following publications of mine: *Foundations of Modern Historical Scholarship* (New York, 1970); "The Rise of Legal History in the Renaissance," *History and Theory* 9 (1970), 174–94; "The Development and Context of Bodin's Method," in *Jean Bodin: Verhandlungen der internationalen Bodin Tagung in München*, ed. H. Denzer (Munich, 1973), 123–50; "Clio and the Lawyers: Forms of Historical Consciousness in Medieval Jurisprudence," *Medievalia et Humanistica*, n.s., 5 (1974), 25–49; "Vico's Road," in *Giambattista Vico's Science of Humanity*, ed. G. Tagliacozzo and D. Verene (Baltimore, 1976), 15–29; and "The Prehistory of Sociology: Montesquieu, Vico and the Legal Tradition," *Journal of the History of the Behavioral Sciences* 16 (1980), 133–44.

36. Alfred Jourdan, *Des Rapports entre le droit et l'économie politique* (Paris, 1885), epigraph.

37. See below, chap. 8.

Notes to Chapter Three

1. Intellectual context is best provided by Maxime Leroy, *Histoire des idées sociales en France*, 3 vols. (Paris, 1947–54). The old survey by Roger Soltau, *French Political Thought in the Nineteenth Century* (Oxford, 1930), is unsatisfactory, and so is the newer one of Dominique Bagge, *Les Idées politiques en France sous la Restauration* (Paris, 1952), at least for the legal tradition.

2. René de Chateaubriand, *Etudes historiques* (Paris, 1831); Louis de Bonald, *Oeuvres* (Paris, 1858), 333.

3. There is a vast specialized literature on these schools (on law, for instance, see below, chap. 6, n. 3), but nothing of great synthetic value.

4. See below, chap. 6, n. 4.

5. François Guizot, *Du Gouvernement de la France depuis la Restauration* (Paris, 1820), 168.

6. Bertier de Sauvigny, *La Restauration* (Paris, 1955), 517.

7. Jean Vidalenc, *La Société française de 1815 à 1848*, vol. 1 (Paris, 1970), 332; cf. D'Herbouville, "Sur l'imputation faite aux Royalists de vouloir rétablir la Dîme et la Féodalité," *Le Conservateur* 1 (1818), 155–67.

8. J. B. Duvergier, *Collection complète des lois*, vol. 25 (Paris, 1838), 78ff.; André Gain, *La Restauration et les Biens des Emigrés* (Nancy, 1929); and see, for example, *Des Biens nationaux, adresse présentée à la chambre des députés de 1816* (Paris, 1816; Bibliothèque Nationale, Lb.⁴⁸680), exemplifying a vast quantity of material on the question, listed in the *Catalogue de l'histoire de France*. See below, chap. 11.

9. Eugène Lerminier, *Au-delà du Rhin*, vol. 1 (Paris, 1835), v. In general see Claude Bellanger et al., *Histoire générale de la presse française*, vol. 2 (Paris, 1969), C. M. Desgranges, *La Presse littéraire sous la Restauration 1815–1830* (Paris, 1907), Irene Collins, *The Government and the Newspaper Press in France 1814–1881* (Oxford, 1959), and Daniel Rader, *The Journalists and the July Revolution in France* (The Hague, 1973).

10. See below, chap. 7.

11. Charles de Rémusat, *Mémoires de ma vie*, ed. C. Pouthas, vol. 2 (Paris, 1958), 138ff. Cf. Paul Janet, *Victor Cousin et son oeuvre* (Paris, 1885), 188ff.; Alan B. Spitzer, "Victor Cousin and the French Generation of 1820," in *From Parnassus, Essays in Honor of Jacques Barzun*, ed. D. Weiner and W. Keylor (New York, 1976), 177–94; Monglond, *Le Préromantisme en France* (Grenoble, 1930), 263ff.; and Sainte-Beuve, *Lundi*, 10 January 1826.

12. See below, chap. 9, n. 4.

13. See David H. Pinkney, *The French Revolution of 1830* (Princeton, 1972), and the criticisms of Thomas H. Beck, *French Legislators, 1800–1834* (Berkeley, 1974), 135ff.; also Henri Tronchon, *Romantisme et Préromantisme* (Paris, 1930).

14. *The Poetry and Prose of Heinrich Heine*, ed. F. Ewen (New York, 1948), 397.

15. Hippolyte Castile, *Les Hommes et les moeurs en France sous le règne de Louis-Philippe*, 2d ed. (Paris, 1853), 6, 188, 199, 378.

16. Saint-Marc Girardin, *Souvenirs et réflexions politiques d'un journaliste* (Paris, 1859), 125.

17. Archibald Young, *An Historical Sketch of the French Bar* (Edinburgh, 1869).

18. See Charles Giraud, *Notice sur Etienne Pasquier* (Paris, 1848), and Sainte-Beuve, *Lundi*, 6 January 1851.

19. Two collections published in *Editions Vilo* (Paris, 1974): *Les Gens de justice* and *Locataires et Propriétaires*.

20. Marcel Rousselet, *La Magistrature sous la Monarchie de Juillet* (Paris, 1937), 9; Saint-Marc Girardin, *Souvenirs*, 84.

21. Rémusat, *Mémoires*, vol. 2, 313. However, in his own *Mémoires*, vol. 2 (Paris, 1855), 136–38, Dupin protested this distortion and told a very different story.

22. François Guizot, *Mémoires*, vol. 1 (London, 1858), 163; and see Sainte-Beuve, "Deux révolutions, l'Angleterre en 1688 et la France en 1830," *Lundi*, 24 August 1830.

23. Chateaubriand, *Etudes historiques*, preface.

24. Jules Michelet, *Oeuvres complètes*, ed. Paul Viallaneix, vol. 2 (Paris, 1972), 217.

25. Heinrich Heine, *Lutèce* (Paris, 1855), 272 (29 July 1842).

26. See now Gabrielle de Broglie, *Histoire politique de la Revue des deux mondes* (Paris, 1979).

27. Louis Blanc, *1848. Historical Revelations* (New York, 1971), 47.

28. See primarily Keith Baker, "The Early History of the Term 'Social Science,' " *Annals of Science* 20 (1964), 211–26, and Leroy, *Histoire des idées sociales*, vol. 2, 13ff.; also Roger Picard, *Le Romantisme social* (New York, 1944), David Evans, *Social Romanticism in France* (New York, 1969), D. G. Charleton, *Secular Religions in France, 1815–1870* (Oxford, 1963), and George Gusdorf, *Les Sciences humaines et la pensée occidentale*, vol. 8, *La Conscience révolutionnaire. Les Idéologues* (Paris, 1978), and vol. 9, *Fondements du savoir romantique* (Paris, 1982).

NOTES TO CHAPTER FOUR

1. Jane Harrison, *Themis* (New York, 1962), 485.

2. For background see my "Gaius Noster: Substructures of Western Social Thought," *American Historical Review* 84 (1979), 619–48.

3. C. G. Hello, *Philosophie de l'histoire de France* (Paris, 1840), 3.

4. See Stanley Mellon, *The Political Uses of History* (Stanford, 1958).

5. In general see *Le Code Civil 1804–1904, Livre du centenaire* (Paris, 1904), especially J. Charmont and A. Chausse, "Les Interprètes du Code Civil," vol. 1, 131–72; A. Esmein, "L'Originalité du Code Civil," vol. 1, 3–21; and R. Saleiller, "Le Code Civil et la méthode historique," vol. 1, 95–129. See also F. Gaudemet, *L'Interprétation du Code Civil en France depuis 1804* (Basel, 1935).

6. P. A. Fenet, *Recueil complet des travaux préparatoires du Code Civil*, vol. 1 (Paris, 1827), 1 (9 August 1793): "Citoyens, elle est enfin arrivée cette époque si desirée qui doit fixer pour jamais l'empire de la liberté et les destinées de la France," referring to "le grand édifice de la législation civile."

7. Cited in B. Schwarz, *The Code Napoleon and the Common-Law World* (New York, 1956), 1.

8. F. A. Trapp, "An Early Photograph of a Lost Delacroix," *Burlington Magazine* 106 (1964), 267–69, (now in George Eastman House, Rochester, N.Y.), photo of an 1855 exhibition, destroyed by fire.

9. Fenet, *Recueil*, vol. 6, 10; cf. Civil Code, art. 1.

10. J. G. Locré, *Esprit du Code Napoléon tiré de la discussion* (Paris, 1805), 1. And yet cf. art. 4: "Le juge qui refusera de juger, sous prétexte du silence, de l'obscurité ou de l'insuffisance de la loi, pourra être poursuivi comme coupable de déni de justice."

11. Napoleon, *Autobiography*, ed. F. Kircheisen (New York, 1931), 240.

12. Fenet, *Recueil*, vol. 2, 20, on art. 5, and Jacques Maleville, *Analyse raisonnée de la discussion du Code Civil* (Paris, 1805), 14.

13. J.B.V. Proudhon, *Cours du droit français* (Dijon, 1809); cf. G. Dumay, *Etude sur la vie et les travaux de Proudhon* (Autun, 1878).

14. Gaudemet, *L'Interprétation*, 13; cf. M. A. Coffinières, *Analyse des nouvelles de Justinien conférées avec l'ancien droit français et le Code Napoléon* (Paris, 1805), 382.

15. See n. 10 above, and in general my "Vera Philosophia: the Philosophical Significance of Renaissance Jurisprudence," *Journal of the History of Philosophy* 14 (1976), 267–79.

16. Fenet, *Recueil*, vol. 1, 11, and J.E.M. Portalis, *Discours*, ed. F. Portalis (Paris, 1844), 2. Cf. Gusdorf, *Les Sciences humaines et la pensée occidentale*, vol. 8 (Paris, 1978), 401.

17. P. N. Riffé-Caubray, *Les Pandectes Françaises*, vol. 1 (Paris, 1803), 5. Cf. A.C.L.M. Biret, *Applications au code civil des Instituts de Justinien et des cinquante livres du Digeste* (Paris, 1824); Coffinières, *Analyse*; H.J.B.

NOTES TO CHAPTER FOUR

Dard, ed., *Code Civil des Français*, 2d ed. (Paris, 1807); G. Leclercq, *Le Droit romain dans ses rapports avec le droit français* (Liege, 1810); and, in general, P. Sagnac, *La Législation civile de la révolution* (Paris, n.d.), 51ff.

18. A. J. Arnaud, *Essai d'analyse structurale du code civil français* (Paris, 1973). Cf. Maleville, *Analyse*, 25, and R. J. Pothier, *Oeuvres*, vol. 6 (Paris, 1831), 210, citing the *Digest*. Roman law connections have been discussed by many early commentators, most notably Riffé-Caubry (1803), Bernardi (1803), Bousquet (1804), Perreau (1805), Locré (1805), Dard (1805), Spangenberg (1808), G. Leclercq (1810), Toullier (1811), Delvincourt (1813), Cotelle (1813), and Biret (1824). In general see, besides the printed catalogue, the photo-reproduced volumes on "jurisprudence" in the reference room of the Bibliothèque Nationale.

19. Chabot d'Allier, *Discours prononcé à l'ouverture du concours pour un cours du droit romain* (Paris, 1819), and L. B. Cotelle, *Discours d'ouverture du cours des Pandectes* (Paris, 1822).

20. Cited by Pieter Geyl, *Napoleon, For and Against*, trans. O. Renier (London, 1949), 79.

21. H. Hayem, "La Renaissance des études juridiques en France sous le Consulat," *Nouvelle revue historique de droit français et étranger* 29 (1905), 96–122 and 378–412, and *Le Code Civil* (see above n. 5), vol. 2, 1111–23; cf. *Annales de législation et de jurisprudence publiées par l'université* 1 and 2 (1802), and *Bulletin de l'Institute de jurisprudence et d'économie politique* 2 (1803); also Michael Fitzsimmons, "Dissolution and Disillusionment: The Parisian Order of Barristers, 1789–1815" (Ph.D. diss., Chapel Hill, 1981).

22. A.A.P. Dupin, *Réflexions sur l'enseignement et l'étude de droit* (Paris, 1807). Cf. J.L.E. Ortolan, *De l'Enseignement du droit en France* (Paris, 1828); A.A.P. Dupin, *Etat actuel de la science du droit romain* (Paris, 1836); and H. Blondeau, *Discours prononcé à la première séance publique du concours ouvert le 10 janvier 1837* (Paris, 1837).

23. *Digest* 1.1.1, and, for instance, J.E.D. Bernardi, *Cours du droit civil* (Paris, 1803), 3.

24. J. Bonnecase, *La Pensée juridique française* (Bordeaux, 1933), including his earlier *L'Ecole de l'exégèse en droit civil* (Paris, 1924). The bibliography of A.A.P. Dupin, *Profession d'avocat*, vol. 2 (Paris, 1830), lists a catechism as well as a verse rendition of the Code.

25. A. M. Demante, "De la manière d'interpréter les lois," in *Programme du cours de droit civil français*, vol. 1 (Paris, 1830), 13.

156

26. P.L.C. Gin, *Analyse raisonnée du droit civil français* (Paris, 1803), on customary as well as Roman law. Cf. my "Guillaume Budé and the First Historical School of Law," *American Historical Review* 72 (1967), 807–34.

27. See Rodolfo Batiza, *Domat, Pothier and the Code Napoléon* (n.p., 1973), showing that over half of the articles were taken from these two authors. Bibliographical details for various works of nineteenth-century legal scholarship can be found in the printed and unprinted catalogues of the Bibliothèque Nationale and (especially for secondary works) in the card catalogue of the Bibliothèque Cujas of the Ecole du Droit.

28. Abel Lefranc, *Histoire du Collège de France* (Paris, 1893), 334.

29. Charles Toullier, *Le Droit civil français suivant l'ordre du Code*, 2d ed., vol. 1 (Paris, 1819), 3ff.; and see below, chap. 5, n. 5.

30. See below, chap. 11, n. 8.

31. M. R. Crussaire, *Analyse des observations des tribunaux de cassation sur le projet de Code Civil* (Paris, 1802), 190. Cf. *Observations du Tribunal de cassation* (Paris, 1802), 7; A.S.G. Coffinières, *Le Code Napoléon expliqué par les décisions suprêmes de la cour de cassation et du conseil d'état* (Paris, 1809); J. Dufour, *Jurisprudence du droit français* (Paris, 1822); T. Crépon, *Cour de cassation* (Paris, 1802), 218ff.; and *Bulletin de la Cour de Cassation*, published from 1796.

32. S. J. Bexon, *Du Pouvoir judiciaire en France et de son inamovibilité* (Paris, 1814), and indeed it appears that passages in this book were censored in this edition despite the restoration of "la liberté de la presse."

33. Henrion de Pansey, *De l'Autorité judiciaire*, in *Oeuvres*, ed. L. Rozet (Paris, 1843). Cf. A. Bardoux, *Les Légistes* (Paris, 1877); F. Ponteil, *Les Institutions de la France de 1814 à 1870* (Paris, 1806), 172ff.; and M. Rousselet, *La Magistrature sous la Monarchie de Juillet* (Paris, 1937).

34. Sainte-Beuve, *Lundi*, 1 March 1852, reviewing the 1844 edition of Portalis, *Discours*. See also Lydie Schimséwitsch (Adolphe), *Portalis et son temps* (Paris, 1936).

35. Mark H. Waddicor, *Montesquieu and the Philosophy of Natural Law* (The Hague, 1970), 126.

36. Portalis, *Discours*, 69, 84, 96. Cf. A. Valette, *De la Durée persistante du droit civil français pendant et depuis la révolution de 1789* (Paris, 1872), and Paul Viard, *Histoire général du droit privé français (1789–1830)* (Paris, 1931).

NOTES TO CHAPTER FIVE

37. Fenet, *Receuil*, vol. 1, 476; cf. A. R. Bousquet, *Explication du Code Civil* (Avignon, 1804), iv.
38. Henri Klimrath, *Travaux sur l'histoire du droit français*, ed. L. A. Warnkönig, vol. 1 (Paris, 1843), 16.
39. Albion Small, *Origins of Sociology* (Chicago, 1924).

NOTES TO CHAPTER FIVE

1. F. F. Poncelet in *Journal des cours publics* (Paris, 1820–21), 3.
2. Cited in Renée Laude, *Henrion de Pansey, 1742–1829* (Lille, 1941), 188.
3. Used here is the fourth edition, A.A.P. Dupin, *Profession d'avocat* (Paris, 1830); cf. A. G. Camus, *Lettres de la profession d'avocat et Bibliothèque choisie des livres de droit*, vol. 1 (Paris, 1818), 7.
4. J. F. Fournel, *Histoire des avocats au Parlement et du Barreau de Paris depuis S. Louis jusqu'au 15 octobre 1790* (Paris, 1813), v, xxvii, and *Histoire du Barreau de Paris dans la cours de la révolution* (Paris, 1816); cf. J.A.J. Gaudry, *Histoire du Barreau de Paris* (Paris, 1864). In general see A. Hiver, *Histoire critique des institutions judiciaires de la France de 1789 à 1848* (Paris, 1848), F. Ponteil, *Les Institutions de la France de 1814 à 1871* (Paris, 1966), and especially J. P. Royer, *La Société judiciaire depuis le XVIIIe siècle* (Paris, 1979).
5. A. J. Tonneau, *Un Jurisconsulte de transition: Charles Toullier (1752-1835) et son temps* (Rennes, 1962), and A. Eon, *Toullier et son temps* (Paris, 1893); cf. X. Desportets, *Notes Biographiques sur la vie et les oeuvres de M. Delvincourt* (Paris, 1832).
6. G. Colmet Daage, *L'Ecole de droit de Paris en 1814, 1815 et 1816* (Paris, 1887). A. Mater, "L'Histoire juridique de la révolution," *Annales révolutionnaires* 11 (1919), 440, speaks of "ces carrières plastiques."
7. H. Gautheron, *Dupin aîné* (Bourges, 1968), and J.L.E. Ortolan, *Notice biographique sur M. Dupin* (Paris, 1840).
8. Dupont and Guichard in the *Globe* 4 (1826), 1.
9. Fournel, *Histoire du Barreau*, 14; [Bernardi], *Observations sur l'ancienne constitution française . . . par un ancien jurisconsulte* (Paris, 1814; Bibliothèque Nationale, Lb.⁴⁵164), 7, 147.
10. Tonneau, *Charles Toullier*, 171.
11. Charles Toullier, *Le Droit civil français*, vol. 3 (Paris, 1819). Cf. Dupin, *Profession d'avocat*, vol. 2, 374; Tonneau, *Charles Toullier*, 72, 77; *Digest* 1.3.37.

158

12. Henrion de Pansey, *Des Biens communaux* and *Justices de paix*, in *Oeuvres judiciaires*, ed. L. Rozet (Paris, 1843), and see above n. 2; also *Eloge de Dumoulin* and *Traité des fiefs*.

13. Henrion, *Oeuvres*, 327.

14. Henrion, *De l'autorité judiciaire*, in *Oeuvres*, 513.

15. Henrion, *Justices de paix*, 1, 106ff. Anonymous judgment in the *Globe* 3 (1826), 35.

16. J.E.D. Bernardi, *Essai sur les révolutions du droit français* (Paris, 1785), and see above, n. 9.

17. J.E.D. Bernardi, *Eloge de Jacques Cujas* (Paris, 1775), and *Essai sur la vie, les écrits et les lois de Michel de L'Hôpital* (Paris, 1807), 151.

18. J.E.D. Bernardi, *Cours de droit civil français* (Paris, 1803), 3, and *Nouvelle théorie des lois civiles* (Paris, 1801), 56. Cf. the curious view of "revolution" taken by La Mothe (*dit* La Hode), *Histoire des révolutions de France* (The Hague, 1738), preface, as "une Entreprise commencée, quoique non achevée, et sans succès."

19. P.L.C. Gin, *Analyse raisonnée du droit françois, Par la comparaison des dispositions des loix Romaines et de celles de la Coutume de Paris, suivant l'ordre des Lois Civiles de Domat* (Paris, 1782), and *Analyse raisonnée du droit françois, Par la comparaison des dispositions des loix Romaines et de celles de la Coutume de Paris, et du nouveau Code des François* (Paris, 1804). There is no modern study of this interesting and versatile scholar.

20. In Dupin, *Profession d'avocat*, vol. 1, 320; and see below, chap. 7, n. 12.

21. A.A.P. Dupin, *Précis historique du droit romain* (Paris, 1809); cf. J. Hillanet, *Evocation du vieux Paris* (Paris, 1952), 500; and see below, chap. 7, n. 12.

22. See now J. L. Thireau, *Charles Dumoulin (1500–1566)* (Geneva, 1972).

23. A.A.P. Dupin, *Eloge des douze magistrats et jurisconsultes composants la galerie de la Cour de Cassation au palais de justice* (Paris, 1836). Other related materials include Antoine Loisel, *Pasquier, ou Dialogue des advocats du Parlement de Paris*, ed. Dupin (Paris, 1844); and cf. *Le Tribunal et la Cour de Cassation, Notice sur le personnel (1791–1879)* (Paris, 1879), including discourses on the legist tradition: Coquille (5 November 1838), Merlin and Proudhon (4 November 1839), Merlin (7 November 1842), Pasquier (6 November 1843), Loisel's *Institutes coutumières* (3 November 1845), on the Cour de Cassation itself, *Olim*,

Portalis, the *Etablissements de Saint Louis*, and (1869) on Professor Troplong.

24. *Ordonnances des Roys de France de la troisième race*, ed. DuLaurier, vol. 1 (Paris, 1723), completed finally with vol. 21, ed. Pardessus (Paris, 1849), and his *Table chronologique* (Paris, 1847); see also below, chap. 8, n. 2. See also L. Halphen, *L'Histoire en France depuis cent ans* (Paris, 1914), chap. 4.

25. J. G. Heineccius, *Elements du droit civil Romain selon l'ordre des Institutes de Justinien*, trans. T. Berthelot (Paris, 1812), and a corrected edition by Charles Giraud (Paris, 1835).

26. René Dussaud, *La Nouvelle Académie des Inscriptions et Belles-Lettres (1795–1914)* (Paris, 1946); also Jürgen Voss, *Das Mittelalter im historischen Denken Frankreichs* (Munich, 1972), and C. Rearick, *Beyond the Enlightenment* (Bloomington, 1974).

27. Heinrich Heine, *Lutèce* (Paris, 1855), 360.

28. Henri Bordier, *Les Archives de la France* (Paris, 1855), 2ff., 15ff.; and on the earliest connections with historiography, see my *Foundations of Modern Historical Scholarship* (New York, 1970), chap. 5.

29. P.C.F. Daunou, *Cours d'études historiques*, vol. 1 (Paris, 1842), 229ff.; see also F. Mignet, *Notes et portraits historiques et littéraires*, 3d ed., vol. 1 (Paris, 1954), 379ff., and Georges Gusdorf, *Les Sciences humaines et la pensée occidentale*, vol. 8 (Paris, 1979).

30. See Stephen A. Kippur, *Jules Michelet* (Albany, 1981), chap. 5.

31. Influential defenses of legal Romanism include Claude Henrys' "Eloge du droit romain," in *Oeuvres*, vol. 1 (Paris, 1738), vi–xxxvii, and in great detail, J. Bouhier, *Observations sur la coutume du Duché de Bourgogne*, vol. 1 of *Oeuvres de jurisprudence* (Dijon, 1787), 353–654.

32. See the informative study of Christian Chêne, *L'Enseignement du droit français en pays de droit écrit (1679–1793)* (Geneva, 1982).

33. Pierre Groseley, *Recherches pour servir à l'histoire du droit françois* (Paris, 1752), vi, 108ff. In general see E. Carcassonne, *Montesquieu et le problème de la constitution française au XVIIIe siècle* (Paris, 1927), René Hubert, *Les Sciences sociales dans l'Encyclopédie* (Paris, 1923), A. Lombard, *L'Abbé Du Bos* (Paris, 1913), and Renée Simon, *Henry de Boullainviller* (Paris, 1942); also Lionel Gossman, *Medievalism and the Ideologies of the Enlightenment* (Princeton, 1968).

34. Marie-Charlotte-Pauline Robert de Lézardière, *Théorie des lois politiques de la monarchie francaise* (Paris, 1844), published from the 1792 edition with the encouragement of Guizot; and C. J. Perreciot,

De l'Etat civil des personnes et de la condition des terres dans les Gaules (Paris, 1845), first published in 1786. Other Old Regime historians were republished in the nineteenth century, including Dubos and Mably (edited by Guizot), but were given little credit by devotees of the new history like Thierry.

35. B. J. Dacier, *Rapport historique sur les progrès de l'histoire et de la littérature ancienne depuis 1789* (Paris, 1810), 272, and M. J. Chenier, *Tableau historique de l'état et des progrès de la littérature française depuis 1789* (Paris, 1818), 59ff.

36. A. J. L'Herbette, *Introduction a l'étude philosophique du droit précédé d'un discours sur les causes de la stagnation de la science de droit en France* (Paris, 1819), ivff.

37. L. Liard, *L'Université de Paris*, vol. 2 (Paris, 1909), 50ff.; Fontaine de Resbecq, *Notice sur le doctorat en droit* (Paris, 1857). The course was taught by F. F. Poncelet, according to *La Thémis* 2 (1820), 397, on which see below, chap. 7.

38. J.L.E. Ortolan, *De l'Enseignement du droit en France* (Paris, 1838).

39. Raymond Troplong, *De le Prescription*, 4th ed., vol. 1 (Paris, 1857), ii, and "De la necessité de restaurer les études historiques applicables au droit français," *Revue de législation et de jurisprudence* 1 (1834), 1-14.

NOTES TO CHAPTER SIX

1. J. G. Fichte, *Addresses to the German Nation*, trans. R. F. Jones and G. H. Turnbill (Chicago, 1922), 107.

2. A. W. Rehberg, *Ueber den Code Napoleon und dessen Einführung in Deutschland* (Hannover, 1814), and cf. Klaus Epstein, *The Genesis of German Conservatism* (Princeton, 1966), 548ff.

3. The best introduction is still Ernst Landsberg's part of Stintzing-Landsberg, *Geschichte der deutschen Rechtswissenschaft*, vol. 3, part 2 (Munich, 1910); also Franz Wieacker, *Privatrechtsgeschichte der Neuzeit* (Göttingen, 1967), 348ff., Guido Fassò, *Storia della filosofia del diritto*, vol. 3 (Milan, 1974), chap. 3, and Peter Stein, *Legal Evolution, The Story of an Idea* (Cambridge, 1980), chap. 3.

4. Forbidden publication in Paris in 1810, Mme de Staël's *De l'Allemagne* appeared in London in 1813. In general see A. Monchoux, *L'Allemagne devant les lettres françaises de 1814 à 1835* (Paris, 1953), I. A. Henning, *L'Allemagne de Mme. de Stael et la polémique romantique* (Paris, 1929), J. M. Carré, *Les Ecrivains français et le mirage allemand*

(Paris, 1947), L. Reynaud, *L'Influence allemande en France au XVIIIe siècle et au XIXe siècle* (Paris, 1921), H. O. Sieburg, *Deutschland und Frankreich in der Geschichtsschreibung des neunzehnten Jahrhunderts* (Wiesbaden, 1951), and G. Cocchiara, *The History of Folklore in Europe*, trans. J. McDaniel (Philadelphia, 1981).

5. Charles de Villers, "Rapport fait à la Classe d'Histoire et de Littérature de l'Institut de France sur l'état actuel de la littérature et d'histoire en Allemagne," in *Essai sur l'esprit et l'influence de la Réformation de Luther* (Paris, 1808).

6. J.E.M. Portalis, *De l'Usage et de l'abus de l'esprit philosophique durant la dixhuitième siècle*, 2d ed. (Paris, 1827); and in general see Henri Tronchon, *La Fortune intellectuelle de Herder à France* (Paris, 1920), and "Entre la Pensée franco-anglaise et la philosophie allemande: les Portalis émigrés et Herder," *Modern Language Notes* 14 (1919), 57–67.

7. F. Portalis, *Du Devoir de l'historien* (Paris, 1800), 129.

8. H. Hayem, "La Renaissance des études juridiques en France sous le Consultant," *Nouvelle revue historique de droit français et étranger* 29 (1905), 96–122.

9. F. Creuzer, *Religions de l'antiquité*, trans. J. D. Guigniaut (Paris, 1825).

10. Victor Cousin, *Introduction to the History of Philosophy*, trans. H. G. Linberg (Boston, 1832), 345ff.; see also Mme Quinet, ed., *Cinquante ans d'amitié, Michelet–Quinet (1825–1875)* (Paris, 1899), Albert Valès, *Edgar Quinet, sa vie et son oeuvre* (Vienne, 1936), Richard Howard Powers, *Edgar Quinet* (Dallas, 1957), Henri Tronchon, *Romantisme et Préromantisme* (Paris, 1930), 78–113, and see below, chap. 9.

11. J. D. Meyer, *Origine et progrès des institutions judiciaires des principaux pays de l'Europe* (Paris, 1818), xixff.

12. Essential texts in J. Stern, *Thibaut und Savigny* (Darmstadt, 1959). See conference "Su Federico Carlo di Savigny," *Quaderni fiorentini per la storia del pensiero giuridico moderno* 9 (1980), and the bibliography compiled by Klaus Luig in *Quaderni fiorentini* 8 (1979), 501–59.

13. Erich Rothaker, "Das Wort 'Historismus,' " *Zeitschrift für deutsche Wortforschung*, n.s., 1 (1960), 4.

14. Recently on this subject, Notker Hammerstein, "Der Anteil des 18. Jahrhunderts an der Ausbildung der historischen Schulen des 19. Jahrhunderts," in *Historische Forschung in 18. Jahrhundert*, ed. Karl Hammer and J. Voss (Bonn, 1976), 432–50, and *Jus und Historie*

(Munich, 1972); also forthcoming by Georg Iggers, "Die Göttinger Historiker und die Geschichtswissenschaft des 18. Jahrhunderts," *Mentalitäten und Lebensverhältnisse, Rudolf Vierhaus zum 60. Geburtstag* (Göttingen, 1983), 385–98.

15. Gustav Hugo, *Lehrbuch des Naturrechts als einer Philosophie des positiven Rechts*, 3rd ed. (Berlin, 1809). See also Arno Buschmann, *Ursprung und Grundlagen der geschichtlichen Rechtswissenschaft, Untersuchungen und Interpretationen zur Rechtslehre Gustav Hugos* (Krefeld, 1963), Jürgen Blühdorn, "Naturrechtskritik und Philosophie des positiven Rechts," *Tijdschrift voor Rechtsgeschiedenis* 45 (1974), 3–17, and Giuliano Marini, *L'Opera di Gustav Hugo nella crisi del giusnaturalismo tedesco* (Milan, 1969).

16. Friedrich Karl von Savigny, *Histoire du droit romain*, translated from 7th ed. by A. Jourdan (Paris, 1825).

17. Hugo, *Lehrbuch*, 4.

18. See especially A. Mazzacane, "Savigny e la storiografia giuridica tra storia e sistema," in *Scritti in onore di Salvatore Pugliatti*, vol. 4 (Milan, 1978), 515–57, and Giuliano Marini, *Savigny e il methodo della scienza giuridica* (Milan, 1966).

19. Friedrich Karl von Savigny, *Vom Beruf unsrer Zeit für Gesetzgebung und Rechtswissenschaft* (Heidelberg, 1814), reprinted in Stern, *Thibaut und Savigny*, 97ff.

20. *Codification Proposal addressed by Jeremy Bentham to All Nations professing Liberal Opinions* (London, 1822).

21. G.W.F. Hegel, *Philosophy of Right*, trans. T. M. Knox (Oxford, 1952), 136.

22. Friedrich Karl von Savigny, *On the Vocation of our Age for Legislation and Jurisprudence*, trans. A. Hayward (London, 1831), 18, 81.

23. See above, chap. 4, n. 6.

24. Savigny, *Vocation*, 22.

25. See below, chap. 7, n. 19.

26. D. R. Kelley, "The Metaphysics of Law: An Essay on the Very Young Marx," *American Historical Review* 83 (1978), 350–67.

27. Quoted by Albion Small, *Origins of Sociology* (Chicago, 1924), 41.

28. K. S. Zachariae, *Versuch einer allgemeinen Hermeneutik des Rechts* (Heidelberg, 1805), and "L'Art d'interpréter les lois," in his *Cours de droit français*, translated and modified by C. Aubry and C. Rau (Strasbourg, 1839), 80ff. Also C. Brocher, "K. S. Zachariae, sa vie et ses oeuvres," *Revue historique de droit français et étranger* 14 (1868),

433–47; 15 (1869), 295–347, 430–89, 557–83. Cf. C. H. Eckhard, *Hermeneutica Juris*, ed. C. W. Walch (Leipzig, 1802). This dimension of hermeneutics is neglected even in the standard survey, Joachim Wach, *Das Verstehen* (Tübingen, 1926); but see F. Geny, *Méthode d'interprétation et sources en droit privé* (Paris, 1899), and Emilio Betti, *Allgemeine Auslegungslehre* (Tübingen, 1967), 438ff., and *Quaderni fiorentini* 7 (1978), devoted to "Emilio Betti e la Scienza giuridica del Novecento"; also D. R. Kelley, "Hermes, clio, Themis," *Journal of Modern History* 55 (1983), 644–68.

29. Friedrich Karl von Savigny, *Traité de droit romain*, trans. C. Guenoux, vol. 1 (Paris, 1840), chap. 4, and Thibaut, *Théorie de l'interprétation logique*, trans. G. de Sandt and A. Mailher de Chassat (Paris, 1811); and see the reviews by A. Vuy and Victor Foucher in *Revue de législation et de jurisprudence* 10 (1839), 221–57.

30. See above, chap. 4, n. 15.

31. J. F. von Schulte, *Karl Friedrich Eichhorn* (Stuttgart, 1884).

32. Jakob Grimm, "Von der Poesie im Recht," *Zeitschrift für geschichtliche Rechtswissenschaft* 2 (1816), 25–99; and see his tribute to Savigny, "Das wort des besitzes," in *Reden und Abhandlungen* (Berlin, 1864), 113–44.

33. See the preface to Michelet, *Histoire de France*, in vol. 3 of *Oeuvres complètes*, 577, and see below, chap. 9, n. 19.

34. J. W. von Goethe, *Conversations with Eckermann*, trans. J. Oxenford (London, 1974), 97.

35. *Cinquante ans d'amitié, Michelet–Quinet*, ed. Mme Quinet (Paris, 1899), October 1836.

36. Saint-Marc Girardin, "Quelques souvenirs sur M. Gans," preface to Eduard Gans, *Histoire du droit de succession en France*, trans. L. de Loménie (Paris, 1845); and see Manfred Riedel, "Eduard Gans als Schüler Hegels," *Rivista di filosofia* 68 (1977), 234–68.

37. Saint-Marc Girardin, *Notices politiques et littéraires sur l'Allemagne* (Paris, 1835), x. Cf. Edgar Quinet, *Allemagne et Italie* (Paris, 1839).

38. Chateaubriand, *Etudes historiques*, 30.

39. See below, chap. 10, n. 4.

40. See below, chap. 8.

NOTES TO CHAPTER SEVEN

1. See Julien Bonnecase, *La Thémis (1819–1831), son fondateur, Athanase Jourdan* (Paris, 1914), later incorporated into his *La Pensée*

juridique. A favorable review appeared in the *Globe* 1 (1824), 403, the same issue in which Thierry's letters on history were printed, though complaining of "un ton que se ressent de l'école"; cf. 3 (1823), 270. Savigny himself supported the effort in a review of *La Thémis* 1 and 2, in *Zeitschrift für geschichtliche Rechtswissenschaft* 4 (1820), 482–90.

2. "Avertissement," *Annales de législation et de jurisprudence* 3 (1822, last issue); cf. *La Thémis* 4 (1822), 475. The translation of Savigny was begun by Meynier in *Annales* 2 (1821), 97ff.

3. Jacques Berriat-Saint-Prix, *Histoire du droit romain suivie de l'histoire de Cujas* (Paris, 1821), reviewed by Hugo in his *Beyträge zur civilistischen Bücherkenntniss*, vol. 2 (Berlin, 1828), 525, and Pelligrino Rossi in *Annales de législation et de jurisprudence* 2 (1821), 383–417.

4. Athanase Jourdan, "Quelques réflections sur l'histoire de la philosophie du droit en France," *La Thémis* 8 (1826), 97–105, especially 114.

5. L. A. Warnkönig, "De l'Etat actuel de la science du droit en Allemagne, et de la révolution qu'elle a eprouvée dans les cours des trente dernières années," *La Thémis* 1 (1819), 1–24. Cf. "De la Science du droit en Allemagne depuis 1815," extracted from *Revue étrangère et française de législation, de jurisprudence et d'économie politique* 9 (1041), and "De l'Enseignement du droit dans les universités d'Allemagne," extracted from *Revue encyclopédique* 39 (1828); also Henri Klimrath, "De l'Etude du droit en Allemagne," *Nouvelle Revue Germanique*, 2d ser., 3 (1831), 43–61, 145–63, 229–59, 309–59.

6. *La Thémis* 8 (1826), 105: "Mais une nouvelle philosophie s'élève; Platon reprend le sceptre des doctrines sociales. Les doctrines platoniciennes seconderont, n'en doutons pas, la nouvelle direction de la jurisprudence, et la France aura aussi sa philosophie de droit."

7. Pelligrino Rossi, "De l'Etude du droit dans ses rapports avec la civilisation et l'état actuel de la science," *Annales de législation et de jurisprudence* 1 (1820), 357–428, especially 432. Cf. Laslo Ledermann, *Pelligrino Rossi* (Paris, 1829), 80, and J. R. de Salis, *Sismondi, 1775–1842* (Paris, 1942).

8. *La Thémis* 2 (1820), 397; 3 (1821), 75; cf. 6 (1824), 203; 8 (1826), 23.

9. *La Thémis* 2 (1820), 383.

10. *La Thémis* 1 (1819), 287; 3 (1821), 16, 402.

11. *La Thémis* 3 (1821), 474: "Les jurisconsultes allemands poursuivent les recherches dont Cujas, Rançonnet, Du Tillet, P. Pithou s'occupent avec tant de succès en France au seizième siècle."

12. *La Thémis* 1 (1819), 94–96, 297–328; 3 (1821), 193–207, 385–

94; 4 (1822), 93, 385; 7 (1825), 165–87; 10 (1830–31), 172–209. Cf. *Civilistische Magazin* 1 (1812), 190–246.

13. *La Thémis* 7 (1825), 165; 10 (1830–31), 161.

14. *La Thémis* 10 (1830–31), 549; and also on the Cujas legend, A.A.P. Dupin, *Profession d'avocat*, vol. 1 (Paris, 1830), 309 (Camus' third letter), and *Etat actuel de la science du droit romain* (Paris, 1836), 16; *Annales de législation et de jurisprudence* 1 (1820), 2; and see above, n. 3 and chap. 4, n. 16.

15. L.F.J. Laferrière, *Histoire du droit civil de Rome et de droit français*, vol. 1 (Paris, 1846), xvii.

16. Edouard Laboulaye, *De l'Enseignement du droit en France* (Paris, 1839), 10; cf. A.A.P. Dupin, *Précis historique du droit romain* (Paris, 1809), 93.

17. *La Thémis* 4 (1822), 304; 6 (1824), 165.

18. *La Thémis* 3 (1821), 367, 380; cf. Hugo's review in *Beyträge*, vol. 2, 426, 534, 544.

19. Warnkönig's summary is in *La Thémis* 3 (1821), 224–35, 445–60; 4 (1822), 234–56; 5 (1823), 345–66, 468–77, and English translation (Edinburgh, 1839). See review by K. S. Zachariae in *Neue Revision der Theorie des römischen Rechts* (Leipzig, 1824), and below, chap. 10, n. 9. Among contemporary French reactions are Guenoux' notice in his translation of Friedrich Karl von Savigny, *Histoire du droit romain à moyen-âge*, vol. 1 (Paris, 1889), and Edouard Laboulaye, *Essai sur la vie et les doctrines de Frédéric Charles de Savigny* (Paris, 1842).

20. *La Thémis* 10 (1830–31), 101–17; 4 (1822), 304–9.

21. "Des procès intentes aux animaux," *La Thémis* 1 (1819), 194–97; cf. 8 (1826), 45–62; Barthélemy de Chasseneux, *Consilia* (Lyon, 1588), 1ff.

22. *La Thémis* 2 (1820), 485–93; 7 (1825), 19–28. See the extraordinary work of Marie-Charlotte-Pauline Robert de Lézardière, first published in 1792, *Théorie des lois politiques de la monarchie française* (Paris, 1844).

23. *La Thémis* 3 (1821), 96–104; 8 (1826), 161–88; cf. L. A. Warnkönig in *Zeitschrift für geschichtliche Rechtswissenschaft* 7 (1831), 52ff.

24. *La Thémis* 3 (1821), 75–92; 6 (1824), 213. See P. H. Templier, *Notice sur la vie et les ouvrages de M. Ducaurroy* (Paris, 1850), and A. M. Demante, "Dupin aîné et Ducauroy," letter to *Revue critique de législation et de jurisprudence (1864)*, in Bibliothèque Nationale, Ln^{27}.42121).

A *PLEIADE* OF LEGAL HISTORIANS

25. A. M. Ducaurroy, *Lettres d'un ancien redacteur de La Thémis à M. Laboulaye . . . sur l'histoire de droit* (Paris, 1846).
26. L. A. Warnkönig, "Der Rechtsgelehrter Dr. Jourdan in Paris und sein Verhältniss zu Reform der Rechtswissenschaft in Frankreich," *Zeitschrift für geschichtliche Rechtswissenschaft* 7 (1831), 43–89, and see Ducaurroy in *La Thémis* 8 (1826), 154–59.
27. See L.F.J. Laferrière, "Introduction historique" to *Tables analytiques de la Revue de législation et de la Revue Critique de législation et de jurisprudence précédées des tables de la Thémis et de la Revue de droit français et étranger* (Paris, 1860).
28. Friedrich Karl von Savigny, *On the Vocation of our Age for Legislation and Jurisprudence*, trans. A. Hayward (London, 1831), 36.

NOTES TO CHAPTER EIGHT

1. See above, chap. 2, n. 25.
2. H. Eloy, *M. Pardessus, sa vie et ses oeuvres* (Paris, 1868). Aside from such brief sketches, *éloges*, or obituary notices, there are no serious studies of any of these five figures. Bibliographical information can be found in these as well as the Bibliothèque Nationale catalogue, and I omit such repetitious references.
3. A.A.P. Dupin, *Profession d'avocat*, vol. 1 (Paris, 1830), 410–22.
4. See above, chap. 2, n. 24.
5. J. M. Pardessus, "Mémoire sur l'origine du droit coutumier en France, et sur son état jusqu'au XIIIe siècle," *Mémoires de l'Institut Royal de France, Académie des Inscriptions et belles-lettres* 10 (1833), 666–765.
6. Victor Molinier, *Eloge sur la vie et les travaux de M. Laferrière* (Toulouse, 1863), and *Eloge de M. F. Laferrière* (Angouleme, 1877).
7. L.F.J. Laferrière, *Histoire du droit civil de Rome et de droit français*, vol. 1 (Paris, 1846), xvi.
8. L.F.J. Laferrière, *Histoire des principes des institutions et des lois pendant la révolution française* (Paris, 1851–52).
9. Henri Klimrath, *Travaux sur l'histoire du droit français*, vol. 1 (Paris, 1843), 113, 146.
10. J. Cabassol, *Charles Giraud* (Aix-en-Provence, 1924), and E. Glasson, *Notice sur la vie et les travaux de M. Charles Giraud* (Paris, 1896).
11. See below, chap. 11, n. 34.
12. Charles Giraud, *Notice sur Etienne Pasquier* (Paris, 1848), 7, and

see his introduction to Etienne Pasquier, *L'Interprétation des Institutes de Justinian*, ed. M. le Duc Pasquier (Paris, 1847); also my *Foundations of Modern Historical Scholarship* (New York, 1970), chap. 10, and Sainte-Beuve, *Lundi*, 6 January 1851.

13. A. Alkan, *Un fondeur en caractères* (Paris, 1866), H. Wallon, *Notice sur la vie et les travaux de M. Edouard Laboulaye* (Paris, 1888), and John Bigelow, *Some Recollections of the Late Edouard Laboulaye* (New York, 1888). Cf. Acton, "German Schools of History," in *Historical Essays and Studies*, ed. J. N. Figgis and R. V. Lawrence (London, 1907), 345.

14. Edouard Laboulaye, *De l'Enseignement du droit en France* (Paris, 1839), 5.

15. Edouard Laboulaye, *Essai sur la vie et les doctrines de Frédéric Charles de Savigny* (Paris, 1842), and see Pierre Legendre, "Lettres de Savigny à Laboulaye," *Zeitschrift der Savigny-Stiftung für Rechtsgeschichte*, Rom. Abt., 88 (1971), 322–28; also below, chap. 11, n. 32.

16. Edouard Laboulaye, "Quelques réflexions sur l'enseignement du droit en France," extracted from *Revue de législation et de jurisprudence* (1845), and *La Chair d'histoire du droit et le concours* (n.p., n.d.). See also his manifestos, "De la Méthode historique en la jurisprudence et de son avenir" and "Introduction," *Revue historique de droit français et étranger* 1 (1855), 1–23.

17. The only study is the introduction of Warnkönig to his edition of Klimrath's *Travaux*, vol. 1.

18. Henri Klimrath, "Essai sur l'étude historique du droit, et son utilité pour l'interprétation du code civil," *Travaux*, vol. 1, 1–62; and on the historical school, articles in *Nouvelle Revue Germanique*, 2d ser., 3 (1831), 43–61, 145–63, 229–59, 309–39.

19. Klimrath, *Travaux*, vol. 1, 113, 146.

20. Klimrath, *Travaux*, vol. 1, 23, 25.

21. A recent survey by C. O. Carbonnel, *Histoire et historiens, 1865–85* (Paris, 1976), is informative social history but without value for present purposes; recourse must still be made to the older manuals of Fueter, Gooch and J. W. Thompson, although they are all silent on the figures treated here.

NOTES TO CHAPTER NINE

1. Jules Michelet, *Oeuvres complètes*, ed. P. Viallaneix, vol. 2 (Paris, 1972), 217. This collection, still in the course of publication, is, along with the editorial notes of Viallaneix, essential for any study of

MICHELET AND THE LAW

Michelet. Despite massive literature, the biography by Gabriel Monod, *La Vie et la pensée de Jules Michelet, 1798–1852* (Paris, 1923), is still unsurpassed; but see also Paul Viallaneix, *La Voie royale* (Paris, 1959).

2. See M. Donzelli, "La Conception de l'histoire de J. B. Vico et son interprétation par J. Michelet," *Annales historiques de la révolution française* 53 (1981), 633–58; Alain Pons, "Vico and French Thought," in *Giambattista Vico, An International Symposium*, ed. G. Tagliacozzo and H. White (Baltimore, 1969), 165–85; E. Tosi, "Vico en France," *Revue de littérature comparée* 11 (1931), 763–77; Armelo D'Amato, *Il Mito di Vico e la filosofia della storia in Francia nella prima metà dell'ottocento* (Naples, 1977); Oscar Haac, *Les Principes inspirateurs de Michelet* (New Haven, 1951); C. Rearick, *Beyond the Enlightenment* (Bloomington, 1974); D. R. Kelley, "Vico's Road: From Philology to Jurisprudence and Back," in *Giambattista Vico's Science of Humanity*, ed. G. Tagliacozzo and D. Verene (Baltimore, 1976), 15–29; and Edmund Wilson, *To the Finland Station* (New York, 1940).

3. Jules Michelet, *Ecrits de jeunesse*, ed. P. Viallaneix (Paris, 1959), 85ff., and *Journal*, ed. P. Viallaneix (Paris, 1959), 51ff.; also *Oeuvres complètes*, vol. 3, 581–601. In general see Werner Kaegi, *Michelet in Deutschland* (Basel, 1936), Ulrich Wyss, *Die wilde Philologie, Jacob Grimm und der Historismus* (Munich, 1979), and W. P. Sohnle, *Georg Friedrich Creuzers "Symbolik und Mythologie" in Frankreich* (Göppingen, 1972).

4. Michelet, *Oeuvres complètes*, vol. 2, 413ff.

5. Pierre-Simon Ballanche, *Essais de palengénésis sociale*, vol. 2 (Paris, 1829), 49–109.

6. Victor Cousin, *Introduction to the History of Philosophy*, trans. H. G. Lindberg (Boston, 1832), 345, and see above, chap. 6, n. 35.

7. Giambattista Vico, *The New Science*, trans. T. G. Bergin and M. H. Fisch (New York, 1961), 22; cf. Michelet, *Oeuvres complètes*, vol. 1, 434.

8. Michelet, *Oeuvres complètes*, vol. 2, 335, 341.

9. Michelet, *Oeuvres complètes*, vol. 2, 603.

10. Michelet, *Oeuvres complètes*, vol. 2, 404.

11. Michelet, *Oeuvres complètes*, vol. 2, 381; vol. 3, 612; and see below, chap. 11, nn. 25 and 38.

12. See above, chap. 3, n. 11.

13. Michelet, *Oeuvres complètes*, vol. 2, 396; cf. *La Thémis* 1 (1819), 496; also T. P. Boulage, *Conclusions sur la loi des Douze-Tables* (Paris, 1804), and on the background Michael Steinberg, "The Twelve Tables and the Question of Origins: An Eighteenth-Century Debate," *Journal of the History of Ideas* 43 (1982), 379–96.

14. Michelet, *Oeuvres complètes*, vol. 3, 629.
15. Michelet, *Oeuvres complètes*, vol. 3, 572 (in preface to *Histoire de France*).
16. Michelet, *Oeuvres complètes*, vol. 3, 567.
17. Michelet, *Journal*, 56.
18. Monod, *Michelet*, 369.
19. Jules Michelet, *Lettres inédits*, ed. Paul Sirven (Paris, 1924), 2 (to Alfred Dumesnil).
20. Michelet, *Oeuvres complètes*, vol. 3, 606.
21. See below, chap. 11, n. 5.
22. Michelet, *Oeuvres complètes*, vol. 3, 606, 649.
23. Michelet, *Oeuvres complètes*, vol. 3, 608, 657.
24. Michelet, *Oeuvres complètes*, vol. 3, 611.
25. Michelet, *Oeuvres complètes*, vol. 3, 697ff.
26. The principal reviews ("dossier") of Michelet's *Origines du droit français* is given by Viallaneix in *Oeuvres complètes*, vol. 3, 836–79; it includes critical appraisals by Martin Doisy in *Revue française*, an anonymous reviewer in *Les Deux Bourgognes*, T. Toussenel in *Le Temps*, Joël Cherbuliez in *Bulletin littéraire et scientifique*, Victor Hennequin in *Le Droit*, Auguste Nisard in *Le Siècle*, L.F.J. Laferrière in *Revue de législation et de jurisprudence*, F. Ozanam in *L'Univers*, M. de la Nourais in *Revue étrangère de législation et d'économie politique*, and P. Haussard in *Revue universelle*.
27. Heinrich Heine, *Lutèce* (Paris, 1855), 272.
28. Saint-Marc Girardin, "Quelques souvenirs sur M. Gans," preface to Gans, *Histoire du droit de succession en France*, trans. L. de Loménie (Paris, 1845), 235.
29. Henri Klimrath, *Travaux*, vol. 1, 150.
30. J. F. Taulier, *Des Progrès de la jurisprudence en France* (Grenoble, 1838), 17.
31. J. P. Chasson, *Essai sur la symbolique du droit, précédé d'une introduction sur la poésie du droit primitif* (Paris, 1847), cxix.
32. Jules Michelet, *The People*, trans. G. H. Smith (New York, 1946), 9ff.
33. Ibid., 27.

NOTES TO CHAPTER TEN

1. A.A.P. Dupin, *Travaux académiques* (Paris, 1862), discourse to the Académie Française, in response to the anonymous judgment in the *Globe* 4 (1826), 35

2. T. P. Boulage, *Principes de jurisprudence française* (Paris, 1819).

3. *Globe* 5 (1827), 509–11, 532; cf. 4 (1826), review of Ducaurroy by "E. L.," and *La Thémis* 8 (1926), 145–53, on the great French legal triumvirate, Cujas, Domat, and Montesquieu.

4. Eugène Lerminier, *De Possessione analytica savignianae* (Paris, 1827). On Lerminier see Bonnie Smith, "The Rise and Fall of Eugène Lerminier," *French Historical Studies* 12 (1982), 377–400.

5. Eugène Lerminier, *Au-delà du Rhin*, vol. 1 (Paris, 1835), 18.

6. *Revue encyclopédique* 64 (1829), 735, probably by Ducaurroy.

7. Eugène Lerminier, *Introduction générale à l'histoire du droit* (Paris, 1829), 270.

8. Eugène Lerminier, *Philosophie du droit*, vol. 2 (Paris, 1831), 311. Cf. Louis de Bonald, *Oeuvres* (Paris, 1858), 333.

9. A. M. Demante, *Programme du cours de droit français*, vol. 1 (Paris, 1830), 13. Cf. "De Interpretatione Codicis," in Ernst Spangenberg, *Institutiones Iuris Civilis Napoleonei* (Göttingen, 1808), chap. 3, and "De l'interprétation des lois," in K. S. Zachariae, *Cours de droit civil français* (Strasbourg, 1839), 71ff.; also F. A. Isambert, "Des Lois interprétatives," *Revue de législation et de jurisprudence* 1 (1834), 241–61.

10. See above, chap. 8, n. 20.

11. Mailher de Chassat, *Traité de l'interprétation* (Paris, 1822), and cf. Delisle, *Traité de l'interprétation* (Paris, 1847–49). The treatise of Crivelli is to be found neither in the Bibliothèque Nationale nor in the Bibliothèque Cujas of the Faculté du Droit.

12. Mailher de Chassat, *Traité*, 2. On the distinction in general see Eduard Gans, *Vermischte Schriften*, vol. 1 (Berlin, 1834), 46, and Pelligrino Rossi, in *Annales de législation et de jurisprudence* 2 (1821), 383–417, and 1 (1820), 31. *La Thémis* 2 (1820), 397, reports a course given at Heidelberg, "Histoire interne de droit civil." The modern analogue is discussed by Thomas Kuhn in *The Essential Tension* (Chicago, 1977), 118–22.

13. François Guizot, *Histoire de la civilisation en France*, 2d ed. (Paris, 1840), 313ff.

14. J. F. Taulier, *Théorie raisonnée du Code Civil* (Grenoble, 1840), and see above, n. 9; also and more generally, H. Blondeau, "Des Méthodes de classification . . . ," *La Thémis* 3 (1821), 246–77. On the systems of Mühlenbruch, Thibaut, Zachariae, and Savigny see W. Belime, *Traité de droit de possession* (Paris, 1842).

15. Alexandre Ledru-Rollin, "De l'influence de l'école française sur le droit au XIXe siècle," introduction to *Jurisprudence Française*

171

(Paris, 1845), and "Réponse de M. ——— à M. Laboulaye," extracted from *Revue de législation* (Bibliothèque Nationale, 8⁰ F. pièce 3621).

16. François Mignet, *Nouveaux éloges historiques*, 2d ed. (Paris, 1878), 7; and see above, chap. 6.

17. Raymond Troplong, *De la Prescription*, vol. 1 (Paris, 1835), xiii.

18. Louis Blanc, *Histoire de dix ans* (Paris, 1882), 1018.

19. See above, chap. 4, n. 18.

20. Lerminier, *Philosophie du droit*, vol. 2, 311.

21. See above, chap. 4, n. 3.

22. P. J. Proudhon, *What is Property?* trans. Benj. R. Tucker (New York, 1966), 85; and cf. *Carnets*, ed. S. Henneguy and J. Fauré-Frement (Paris, 1966).

23. Proudhon, *What is Property?* 77. Among Proudhon's targets, besides Thiers, Cousin, and Old Regime authors like Pothier, were most of the great names of contemporary jurisprudence, including Toullier, Duranton, Troplong, Laboulaye, and, of course, his cousin, the elder Proudhon.

24. Eduard Gans, *Ueber die Grundlage des Besitzes, eine Duplik* (Berlin, 1839), and see my article, "The Metaphysics of Law," cited above, chap. 6, n. 26. Other entries in this debate are listed by Rudorff in the seventh edition of Savigny's *Das Recht des Besitzes* (Berlin, 1865).

25. Karl Marx, "The Philosophical Manifesto of the Historical School of Law," in *Collected Works*, vol. 1 (New York, 1976), 203–10; and see Christoph Schefold, *Die Rechtsphilosophie des jungen Marx von 1842* (Munich, 1970), and Hasso Jaeger, "Savigny and Marx," *Archives de philosophie du droit* 12 (1967), 65–89. In general Marx follows the argument of Hegel, *Grundlinien der Philosophie des Rechts* in *Werke* (Frankfurt-am-Main, 1970), 102ff.

26. Pelligrino Rossi, *Cours d'économie politique* (Paris, 1840), 34; cf. *Mélanges d'économie politique, d'histoire et de philosophie*, vol. 2 (Paris, 1857), 18.

27. Karl Marx, "Contribution to the Critique of Hegel's Philosophy of Law," in *Collected Works*, vol. 3, 181.

NOTES TO CHAPTER ELEVEN

1. P. J. Proudhon, *What is Property?* trans. Benj. R. Tucker (New York, 1966), 52.

2. Adolphe Thiers, *De la propriété* (Brussels, 1849), 9. For a fuller discussion in the social context see the article by Bonnie Smith and me, "What was Property? Legal Dimensions of the Social Question in France, .1789-1848." *Proceedings of the American Philosophical Society* 128 (1984), 200–30.

3. Jules Michelet, *The People*, trans. G. H. Smith (New York, 1946), 29.

4. See James Tully, *A Discourse of Property: John Locke and His Adversaries* (Cambridge, 1980), Richard Teichgraeber, "Hegel on Property and Poverty," *Journal of the History of Ideas* 38 (1977), 47–64, and more generally Richard Schlatter, *Private Property, The History of an Idea* (London, 1951).

5. See D. R. Kelley, "Gaius Noster: Substructures of Western Social Thought," *American Historical Review* 84 (1979), 619–48.

6. T. Chavot, *Traité de la propriété mobilière*, vol. 1 (Paris, 1839), 217. In general see Michel Vidal, "La Propriété dans l'école de l'exégèse en France," *Quaderni fiorentini* 5/6 (1976–77), 7–40.

7. J. G. Locré, *Esprit du Code Napoléon*, vol. 1 (Paris, 1805), 52.

8. Raymond Troplong, *De la Propriété d'après le Code Civil* (Paris, 1848), 7.

9. A. R. Bousquet, *Explication du Code Civil*, vol. 2 (Avignon, 1804), 29.

10. Charles Toullier, *Le Droit civil français*, vol. 2 (Paris, 1819), 46.

11. J.E.M. Portalis, *Discours*, ed. F. Portalis (Paris, 1844), 209.

12. Toullier, *Le Droit civil français*, vol. 2, 26; and see Jean Belin, *La Logique d'une idée-force: L'Idée d'utilité sociale et la révolution française (1789–1792)* (Paris, 1939).

13. Toullier, *Le Droit civil français*, vol. 1, 251; and see above all André Gain, *La Restauration et les Biens des Emigrés* (Nancy, 1929).

14. C. Reinhold Noyes, *The Institution of Property* (New York, 1936), 49.

15. Friedrich Karl von Savigny, *Das Recht des Besitzes*, 7th ed. (Berlin, 1865), with a bibliographical appendix of sources and nineteenth-century reactions. Writes Eugen Ehrlich in *Fundamental Principles of the Sociology of Law*, trans. W. Moll (New York, 1962), 320: "I have gained the conviction in my travels that in the literature of the world there is not another monograph the name of which and, in part, the content of which is so well known to the jurists of each and every legal system as Savigny's *De Possessione*. It is the true *Programmschrift* (program book) of the Historical School for practical juristic sci-

ence." See also Brutti, "L'Intuizione della proprietà nel sistema di Savigny," *Quaderni fiorentini* 5/6 (1976–77), 41–104.

16. Portalis, *Discours*, 212.

17. R. T. Troplong, *De la Prescription*, vol. 1 (Paris, 1835), 361.

18. J. M. Carou, *Traité théoretique et practique des actions possessoires*, 2d ed. (Paris, 1841), 3.

19. Louis Dunod, *Traités des prescriptions, de l'alienation des biens de l'église et des dixmes* (Dijon, 1730), iv, 15.

20. Edouard Laboulaye, *Histoire du droit de propriété foncière en occident* (Paris, 1839), 59; cf. Molitor, *La Possession* (Paris, 1868), 3, and Troplong, *De la Prescription*, vol. 1, 374.

21. J.E.D. Bernardi, *Cours de droit civil français*, vol. 1 (Paris, 1803), 236–42. Cf. Ronald Meek, *Smith, Marx and After* (London, 1977), 20ff.

22. Toullier, *Le Droit civil français*, vol. 2, 42ff.

23. Carou, *Traité théoretique*, 9–13.

24. Savigny, *Das Recht des Besitzes*, passim, citing *Digest* 41.1.2.1; and cf. below, n. 29.

25. B. G. Niebuhr, *Histoire romaine*, vol. 2, trans. Golbérg (Paris, 1830), 97ff., 312.

26. Carou, *Traité théoretique*, 17.

27. W. Belime, *Traité du droit de possession* (Paris, 1842), viii, 5.

28. J. F. Taulier, *Théorie raisonnée du Code Civil* (Grenoble, 1840).

29. Troplong, *De la Prescription*, vol. 1, 383; Molitor, *La Prescription*, 3. *Digest* 41.2.1.1: "dominium rerum ex naturali possessione coepisse."

30. Troplong, *De la Prescription*, vol. 1, 16, and *De la Propriété*, 16, citing Michelet.

31. Troplong, *De la Prescription*, vol. 1, 8. Cf. A. J. Arnaud, *Essai d'analyse structurale du code civil français, La Règle du jeu dans la paix bourgeoise* (Paris, 1973).

32. Nicolas Bergasse, *Essai sur la propriété* (Paris, 1821), and Gain, *La Restauration*, vol. 1, 441–54, 473.

33. See above, chap. 10, n. 22.

34. Charles Giraud, *Recherches sur le Droit de Propriété chez les Romains* (Aix, 1838), 3, 58.

35. Laboulaye, *Histoire du droit de propriété*, 62, 59.

36. Portalis, *Discours*, 210.

37. Giraud, *Recherches*, 9.

38. Paolo Grossi, *"Un Altro modo di possedere"* (Milan, 1977). Marx, referring to Niebuhr, extended the concept of *ager publicus* and incorporated it into his own technical terminology, in, for example, *Pre-Capitalist Economic Formations*, trans. J. Cohen (London, 1965), 74, and *The Ethnological Notebooks*, ed. Lawrence Krader (Assen, 1972).

39. Proudhon, *What is Property?* 258.

40. P. J. Proudhon, *Théorie de la propriété* (Paris, 1871), 6. In general see Antonio Zanfarino, "La proprietà nel pensiero di Proudhon," *Quaderni fiorentini* 5/6 (1976–77), 165–200, and K. Stoyanovitch, "Les Biens selon Marx," *Archives de Philosophie du droit* 24 (1979), 197–212.

41. Jules Michelet, *Origines du droit français* (Paris, 1839), and see above, chap. 9. In general see Alfons Dopsch, *The Economic and Social Foundations of European Civilization*, trans. M. G. Beard and N. Marshall (New York, 1937), chap. 1, and Carl Stephenson, "The Problem of the Common Man in Early Medieval Europe," *American Historical Review* 51 (1946), 419–38.

42. Proudhon, *What is Property?* 335ff.

43. Michelet, *The People*, chap. 1.

44. See Marx, *The Ethnological Notebooks*, and my article, "The Science of Anthropology: An Essay on the Very Old Marx," forthcoming in *Journal of the History of Ideas*.

45. Fustel de Coulanges, "Le Problème des origines de la propriété foncière," in *Questions historiques*, ed. C. Jullian (Paris, 1893), and more generally Emile de Lavelaye, *Primitive Property*, trans. G. Marriott (London, 1878).

NOTES TO CHAPTER TWELVE

1. See above, chap. 1, n. 1.

2. Richard Glasser, *Time in French Life and Thought*, trans. C. G. Pearson (Manchester, 1972), 259.

3. L.F.J. Laferrière, *Histoire du droit civil de Rome*, vol. 1 (Paris, 1846), xvi, and see above, chap. 11, n. 18.

4. Frank Manuel, *The Prophets of Paris* (Cambridge, Mass., 1962).

5. Cited by Karl Löwith, *From Hegel to Marx*, trans. D. Green (New York, 1964), 5.

6. See Jean Vidalenc, *La Société française de 1815 à 1848* (Paris, 1970), and Roger Price, *The French Second Republic, A Social History*

(London, 1972); also Terry Clark, *Prophets and Patrons* (Cambridge, Mass., 1973), 125ff.

7. Lorenz von Stein, *The History of the Social Movement in France*, trans. K. Mengelberg (Totowa, N.J., 1964).

8. P. J. Proudhon, *Carnets*, ed. S. Henneguy and J. Fauré-Fremet (Paris, 1960), 38.

9. See above, chap. 10, n. 27.

10. Proudhon, *Carnets*, vol. 2, 66. Cf. Etienne Dumont, *From Mandeville to Marx* (Chicago, 1977), and in general Lucette Le Van-Lemesle, "La Promotion de l'économie politique en France au XIXe siècle jusqu'à son introduction dans les facultés," *Revue d'histoire moderne et contemporaine* 27 (1980), 270–94.

11. *Journal des économistes* 20 (1848), 113.

12. Brief discussion in J. W. Thompson, *A History of Historical Writing*, vol. 2 (New York, 1942), 410ff., and more generally Joseph Schumpeter, *A History of Economic Analysis* (New York, 1954).

13. Wilhelm Röscher, starting with *Grundriss zu Vorlesungen über die Staastwirthschaft. Nach geschichtlicher Methode* (Göttingen, 1843).

14. Emile Levasseur, *Histoire des classes ouvrières en France depuis la conquête de Jules César jusqu'à la révolution* (Paris, 1859).

15. Anselm Batbie, *Nouveau Cours d'économie politique* (Paris, 1866), 9.

16. Henri Baudrillart, *La Propriété* (Paris, 1867), 6, 15.

17. This connection is lost sight of in many allegedly historical discussions of modern anthropology; exceptions are Murray J. Leaf, *Man, Mind and Science* (New York, 1979), and less surprisingly, Leopold Pospisil, *Anthropology of Law* (New York, 1971). The naturalistic divergence of French anthropology is discussed by Clark, *Prophets and Patrons*, 116ff.

18. Louis Halphen, *L'Histoire en France depuis cent ans* (Paris, 1914), chap. 4.

19. Proudhon, *Carnets*, vol. 1, 37.

20. Léon Duguit, *Les Transformations générales du droit privé depuis le Code Napoléon* (Paris, 1912), and cf. E. Gaudemet, *L'Interprétation du Code Civil en France depuis 1804* (Basel, 1935), 56ff.

21. Emile de Lavelaye, "Des Rapports de l'économie politique avec la morale, le droit et la politique," *Revue des Deux Mondes* 48, no. 3 (1878), 917, and Duguit, *Les Transformations*, 147.

22. Ernest Renan, *L'Avenir de la Science, Pensées de 1848* (Paris, n.d.), 126ff.

23. Ibid., 161-63.

24. See William R. Keylor, *Academy and Community, The Foundation of the French Historical Profession* (Cambridge, Mass., 1975).

25. Saint-Beuve, *Lundi*, 13 December 1830.

INDEX

Acton, Lord, 3, 6, 17, 18, 27
Ampère, J. J., 35
Annales de législation et de jurisprudence, 85, 86, 87, 124
Arbois de Jubainville, H., 100
Archives philosophiques, 102
Assizes of Jerusalem, 88, 94
Augustine, 109
Ayrault, Pierre, 89

Babbitt, Irving, 23
Babouvism, 31
Bachofen, J. J., 145
Bacon, Francis, 116
Baker, Keith, 7
Ballanche, P. S., 24, 102, 110
Barante, Prosper de, 20, 22, 34, 38, 93
Bartolus, 47
Batbie, Anselme, 144
Baudrillart, Henri, 144
Beaumanoir, Philippe de, 63, 66
Belime, W., 133
Bentham, Jeremy, 42, 54, 70, 77, 85, 89
Béranger, P. J. de, 32
Bernardi, J.E.D., 60, 63, 64, 132
Berriat-Saint-Prix, Jacques, 65, 86, 88, 89, 90
Beugnot, Arthur, 110
Biener, F. A., 89
Blackstone, William, 49
Blanc, Louis, 38, 39, 120
Blanqui, Auguste, 143
Blondeau, H., 46
Bodin, Jean, 62, 89
Bonald, L.G.A. de, 16, 26, 32, 115, 141

Bonapartism, 7, 16, 25, 28, 29, 39, 43, 60, 65, 69, 80, 130
Boucher d'Argis, A.J.B., 57, 68
Bouhier, J., 68, 69
Boulage, T. P., 119
Boullainvilliers, Henri de, 63, 68
Bousquet, A. R., 129
Bracton, 108
Burke, Edmund, 16, 29, 30, 32, 64
Butterfield, Herbert, 3, 22

Cambacérès, J.J.R. de, 45, 47, 64, 78
Campanella, Tommaso, 136, 138
Camus, A. G., 15, 16, 54, 56, 57, 59, 65, 66, 113
Carbonari, 30, 31, 32, 41
Carou, J. M., 131, 132, 133, 140
Chabot d'Allier, G. A., 46
Charles IX, 32, 36, 38, 67
Charter of 1815, 31, 32, 50, 56
Chassan, J. P., 110
Chasseneux, Barthélemy de, 90
Chateaubriand, René de, 6, 16, 17, 18, 19, 21, 24, 27, 32, 35, 38, 69, 72, 83, 116, 139, 147
Chenier, André, 106
Chenon, Emile, 100
Chevalier, Michel, 143, 144
Cicero, 75
Civil Code, 12, 25, 31, 33, 42–49, 51, 53, 54, 56, 57, 60, 64, 65, 68, 71, 73, 74, 77, 78, 80, 81, 88, 96, 97, 98, 110, 115, 117, 119, 120–23, 125, 127, 129, 130, 134, 136, 141, 142
Civilistisches Magazin, 76
Codification, 54, 55, 77–80, 87, 89, 98

179

INDEX

Portalis, J.E.M., 45, 51–54, 65, 68, 73, 74, 78, 93, 95, 120, 131, 136, 140
Positivism, 39, 146
Pothier, R. J., 49, 60, 66, 71, 78, 96, 116, 121
Proudhon, J.B.V., 44, 47, 48, 121, 136
Proudhon, P. J., 25, 111, 121–27, 131, 132, 135, 136, 137, 142, 143, 145
Prussian Code, 55, 78, 122, 123
Pufendorf, Samuel, 49
Pütter, J. S., 73, 76, 87

Quinet, Edgar, 35, 46, 74, 83, 101, 103, 106, 111

Ranke, Leopold, 8, 11, 75, 140, 148
Rehberg, A. W., 73, 77
Rémusat, Charles, 35
Renan, Ernest, 146, 147
"resurrection," 12, 13, 14, 27, 67, 102
Revue de législation et de jurisprudence, 91, 92, 95
Revue des deux mondes, 39, 114, 147
Revue des questions historiques, 147
Revue encyclopédique, 34, 113
Revue Foelix, 91
Revue française, La, 34
Revue historique, 147, 148
Revue historique de droit français et étranger, 95, 97
Revue Wolowski, 91
Robespierrism, 17, 53
Robinson, J. H., 3
Roman law, 42–49, 64, 65, 68, 75, 76, 77, 80, 83, 88, 91, 95, 96, 102–7, 128, 130, 131
Romanticism, 4, 11, 23, 26–29, 35, 141
Röscher, Wilhelm, 143

Rossi, Pelligrino, 39, 85, 86, 87, 124, 125, 143
Rousseau, J. J., 23, 29, 53, 57, 108, 136

Saint-Simon, C. H. de, 21, 31, 39, 114, 120
Sainte-Beuve, C. A., 13, 18, 27, 31, 35, 39, 53, 65, 96, 114, 115, 147, 148
Salian law, 94, 141
Sarazin, Jean, 13, 18, 27
Savigny, Friedrich Karl von, 12, 54, 63, 65, 73, 75–83, 85–89, 91, 92, 95–99, 113–19, 122, 123, 124, 130–34, 136, 137
Schelling, F. von, 72
Schleiermacher, Friedrich, 80, 81
Schlosser, F. C., 98
Schlözer, Ludwig, 76
Schmidt, P. A., 73
Scott, Walter, 6, 18, 35
Seidensticker, J.A.L., 74
Seyssel, Claude de, 22, 64, 96
Shakespeare, William, 35
Sicardus, 78
Siéyès, E. J., 19, 22
Sismondi, J.C.L. de, 85, 86, 109, 124
Small, Albion, 55
Smith, Adam, 132
"social," 4, 25, 26, 30, 33, 40, 41, 45, 87, 115, 120, 121, 141, 146
Société de l'Histoire de France, 20, 66
Sorokin, Pitrim, 3
Spangenberg, Ernst, 65, 71, 81
"spirit of the laws," 44, 53, 81, 82, 102
Spittler, Ludwig von, 76, 87
Staël, Mme de, 17, 30, 69, 72, 73, 75, 83, 114
Stahl, F. J., 98

183

Library of Congress Cataloging in Publication Data

Kelley, Donald R.
Historians and the law in postrevolutionary France.

Bibliography: p.
Includes index.
1. Law—France—History and criticism. 2. France—
History—1789–1815—Historiography. I. Title.
LAW   349.44'09   84–42577

ISBN 0–691–05428–2 (alk. paper) 344.4009